Designing Management Information Systems

Designing
Management
Information
Systems

Hans van der Heijden

OXFORD

UNIVERSITY PRESS

OXFORD
UNIVERSITY PRESS

Great Clarendon Street, Oxford ox2 6DP

Oxford University Press is a department of the University of Oxford.
It furthers the University's objective of excellence in research, scholarship,
and education by publishing worldwide in

Oxford New York

Auckland Cape Town Dar es Salaam Hong Kong Karachi
Kuala Lumpur Madrid Melbourne Mexico City Nairobi
New Delhi Shanghai Taipei Toronto

With offices in

Argentina Austria Brazil Chile Czech Republic France Greece
Guatemala Hungary Italy Japan Poland Portugal Singapore
South Korea Switzerland Thailand Turkey Ukraine Vietnam

Oxford is a registered trade mark of Oxford University Press
in the UK and in certain other countries

Published in the United States
by Oxford University Press Inc., New York

British Library Cataloguing in Publication Data

Data available

Library of Congress Cataloging in Publication Data

Data available

Typeset by SPI Publisher Services, Pondicherry, India
Printed in Great Britain
on acid-free paper by
the MPG Books Group

ISBN 978–0–19–954632–9 (Hbk.)
ISBN 978–0–19–954633–6 (Pbk.)

1 3 5 7 9 10 8 6 4 2

☐ PREFACE

Management information systems produce the information that managers use to make important strategic decisions. They form the basis for management reports, both financial and non-financial, and as such they are a vital component of modern business management. Few managerial decisions are taken without consulting the data captured by management information systems.

This book covers the essential managerial skills that are necessary to design these systems. It is written for managers, those studying business management, and those developing management information systems on behalf of management.

I was motivated to write this book because many managers are, in my experience, rather poor designers of their own management reports. They often struggle to make full use of the data that is available to them. It is true that many use management information systems in one form or another, usually implemented through a series of spreadsheets. Indeed some have access to very sophisticated 'business intelligence' systems. Yet these spreadsheets (and their sophisticated counterparts) are often ill-organized, and tend to obfuscate rather than enlighten. In addition, there is not a great deal of material available for those managers wishing to improve their skills in designing management information systems. The existing books on information systems often emphasize the technological rather than the managerial aspects.

This book aims to address these issues. In writing it I have firmly adopted the managerial perspective, and I have not aimed to compromise for the benefit of the more technically minded. You will find few references to specific information technologies in this book, because this book is not about technology. You will not have to be, indeed ought not to be, a computer programmer to be able to benefit from this book.

Three core assumptions form the basis of this book and I should like to summarize them here.

Information systems and information technology: It is important to remember that information systems and information technology are distinct concepts. Information technology is the *carrier* of data and information systems are applications designed to make sense of that data. I realize this is a rather trivial statement for many, but it is often forgotten and I do not mind repeating it here. Too often managers equate information systems with information technology and withdraw from the subject as a consequence.

Preventing information overload: Much discussion on the design of management information systems should revolve around the prevention of information overload. Information processing skills are essential to deal with information overload, and they should be used to inform and shape the design of the management information system. I believe it is important that we elevate the status of these information processing skills, and that we place them firmly in the required toolkit of any manager.

Supporting management decisions: My third assumption is that it is important not to lose sight of the managerial decisions for which we are collecting data and designing systems. Any management information system needs to make clear what purpose it serves, and what types of decisions it will support. If we cannot make this clear, the information system will be useless.

The first part of this book is orientated towards developing key transferable skills to deal with managerial information. I will be focusing on four competences: structuring data, querying data, aggregating data, and visualizing data. Together I believe these competences form the core information processing toolkit that I would encourage any manager to study.

In the second part of the book, I will cover two major types of managerial decisions: the monitoring of key performance indicators and the selection of alternatives from a list of available options. These are the decisions for which management information systems can play a particularly helpful role, and I am covering them in some detail to emphasize that we need to design management information systems for specific types of managerial decisions.

In writing this book, I was fortunate enough to enjoy the constructive feedback from three colleagues and friends, and I should like to acknowledge them here: Thomas Acton, Thomas Chesney, and Daniel Goersch. They have spotted many errors in earlier drafts of this book. Any remaining errors are, of course, my own. Finally, my thanks go to Maddy and to my family for their love and support throughout.

United Kindgom   Guildford
May 2008

CONTENTS SUMMARY

⬜ CONTENTS

☐ LIST OF FIGURES

☐ LIST OF TABLES

1 Management information systems

KEY CONCEPTS

Data	Management information system
Information	Transaction processing system
Information system	Information overload

KEY THEMES

When you have read this chapter, you should be able to define those key concepts in your own words, and you should also be able to:

1. Explain the differences between transaction systems and management information systems.

2. Outline a range of forms in which management information systems are commercially available.

3. Discuss the role of information overload in the design of management information systems.

1.1. **Introduction**

To start off this book I shall first provide a broad introduction to a number of important terms and concepts. I will cover some basic definitions of data, information, and information systems, and then discuss the differences between transaction processing systems and management information systems. This will enable us to discuss the configurations of transaction and management systems that are commonly in use in organizations.

The design process also needs a few introductory words, as it often means different things to different people. I shall discuss the different views of design and point out the one that is adopted in this book.

An important and recurring concept in this book is the concept of information overload. It is important because our designs will always have to guard against the threat of information overload. Also, all information processing skills deal with the reduction of information overload in some form or another. We shall be referring to the concepts of information overload frequently in the remainder of this book, and I will introduce it in this chapter too.

The last part of this chapter contains an overview of the chapters of this book. As I intend to use a single case to illustrate the issues and concepts, I shall also introduce that case at the end of this chapter.

1.2. Management information systems defined

Before we can discuss the design of management information systems, we need to go through a number of terms and definitions. These are essential to understand the rest of the material.

First of all, the definitions of data and information. *Data* refers to raw facts that describe a particular phenomenon. For example, the amount of sales generated by a particular sales agent on a particular day is data. The number of television programmes that you watch on any particular evening is data. Your favourite colour is data. The word 'data' is often treated as singular but it is actually plural. The correct singular form for data is *datum* (Latin for a given, a fact). Datum is rarely used, which is a bit unfortunate because linguistically it would be more precise to refer to a single fact as a datum, and to a set of facts as data.

Information, then, is data that has a particular meaning in a particular context (Laudon and Laudon 2004; Haag, Cummings, and Phillips 2007). For example, if I want to know the sales performance of a particular sales agent, the volume of sales generated by that agent would be information for me. Your favourite colour would not. On the other hand, if I wanted to give you a birthday gift, your favourite colour would be information for me and the sales data would not (presumably). You see that the context gives the data its meaning, and that data can turn into information depending on the context.

Let us move on to the definition of an information system as used in this book. An *information system* is a set of interrelated components that collect (or retrieve), process, store, and distribute information to support decision-making in an organization (Laudon and Laudon 2004). So, an information system takes data as input, and processes it into output information for the benefit of decision-making.

There is another set of information system definitions which uses the term 'system' a bit more liberally (e.g. Haag et al. 2007). Those definitions count not only hardware and software components as part of the system but also the people that collect the data and the processes that they carry out. In this sense, an entire organization can be viewed as one big information system, processing data from the environment into information for the benefit of, say, the management. To avoid any confusion between the two types of definitions, we shall avoid these more inclusive definitions of information systems in this book.

The systems that we shall talk about in this book are classified as *formal* information systems, that is, they rest on accepted and fixed definitions of data and procedures for collecting, sorting, processing, disseminating, and using these data (Laudon and Laudon 2004). The data that I will describe is structured, and the processes that shape the data into information are also structured. Contrast this to *informal* information systems, which rely on unstructured definitions of data: anecdotal customer feedback and office gossip would be good examples. Most managers would argue that the informal system is as important as the formal one, indeed many would argue it is the most important. In any case it is useful to understand the distinction between these two types, and to appreciate the use of both in management decision-making.

Finally, a *management information system* is an information system that provides output to a manager. The term 'manager' refers to decision-makers in organizations only, which is admittedly a somewhat narrow view of the concept, but it is the one we shall be using in this book. This is of course not to suggest that management information systems cannot be developed to manage other things, say, your personal wealth.

1.3. **Types of systems**

A distinction is often made between management information systems and transaction processing systems.

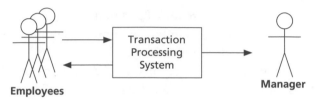

Figure 1 TPS/MIS configuration 1. Arrows indicate flow of data

Transaction processing systems are those systems that provide support to the operations of the organization. Data such as sales orders, production orders, and accounting data is input into these systems on a daily basis. The data is then used to provide information to other employees working in the organization. For example, the sales department enters sales orders into the transaction processing system. The finance department uses this data to generate an invoice. The accounting department uses this data to update the organization's general ledger. The focus in these systems is thus often on capturing data, and on using that data to run the operations of the organization.

In contrast to these transaction processing systems, *management information systems* provide support for tactical and strategic decisions. The information that these systems provide will not affect operations in the short term, but will form the basis for longer-term decisions, with broader and wider implications for operations. The focus in these systems is thus on summarizing and analysing transaction data, for the benefit of effective managerial decision-making.

In many small organizations, the transaction processing system doubles as the management information system. Although not exclusively designed for management purposes, most transaction processing systems do provide a wide range of management reports. Managers then use the same system as the employees, often at the same time. Figure 1 visualizes this configuration.

This works well for organizations and departments of small size, but it quickly gets out of control when the organization grows and the volume of transaction data increases as a consequence. This is for two reasons. The first reason is that the data in the transaction processing system can become very volatile. The system is often used by many employees, who continuously update the system with the latest information. It is thus

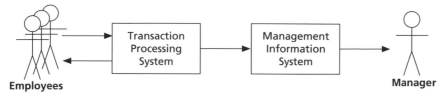

Figure 2 TPS/MIS configuration 2. MIS separated from TPS

entirely possible that a manager sets aside time to analyse the data from the system, and finds that by the end of the analysis the underlying data is already different from the one at the start.

The second reason is more of a technical nature. A manager will often want to look at transaction data in different ways. Say, for example, we want to look at sales revenue by country, by sales team, and by customer. All these reports require computing processing power, which can sometimes (in the case of thousands of sales orders) be very significant. So much so that the manager starts to severely slow down the performance of the information system while it is in use by other employees.

It is for both reasons that the data set for transaction processing systems and the data set for management information systems are often separated. We make a snapshot of the data that is in the transaction processing system, and use that snapshot as the basis for our management information system. Management information systems are thus often *read-only* systems, using a copy of the transaction data to analyse and study. Figure 2 visualizes this configuration.

A benefit of the introduction of an intermediate step between transaction data and management data is that we can use the 'in-between' stage to merge data from several transaction processing systems. For example, if we had a separate sales system and a separate inventory system, we could combine data about sales orders and data about inventory levels to identify gaps between what sells well and what the organization still has in stock.

In organizations with very large transactional data sets, an entirely new data set is often created in preparation for the management information system. It is common to refer to that intermediary data set as a *data ware-house*. We shall refer to the 'incoming' transaction processing systems as *source systems*, in that they provide the source data for the data warehouse. Figure 3 visualizes this configuration.

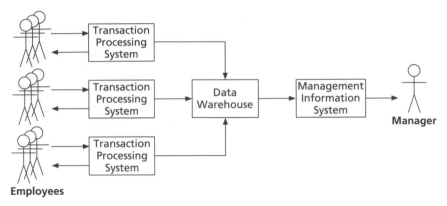

Employees

Figure 3 TPS/MIS configuration 3. Introduction of data warehouse

I do certainly not want to give the impression that this process of transferring data from one system to another is easy and straightforward. In fact, I hope that by the end of this book you will appreciate how complex and difficult this transformation can actually be. Problems can arise, for example, when there is a time lag between the transfer of data, in which case the management information is not entirely up to date. It is also possible that the data structures from the source systems are not quite equal to the data structures from the management information system, in which case a mapping needs to be made. Such a mapping may not always be satisfactory. Commercial system vendors pay substantial attention to the interfaces between transaction and management systems, and many management information system providers have standard interfaces to gain access to widely used transaction processing systems.

Two related terms that you sometimes encounter, and that warrant mention here, are *OLTP* and *OLAP*. OLTP stands for *Online Transaction Processing* and OLAP stands for *Online Analytical Processing*. These terms were introduced several years ago to differentiate between transaction processing systems and management systems.

I have already mentioned commercial vendors of management information systems. It is important to realize that transaction processing systems and management information systems come in many different shapes and sizes. Below I want to set out a number of common forms in which these are commercially available.

Spreadsheet: *Spreadsheets* are software applications that organize data into worksheets: free-format, table-like structures with rows and columns. The data is captured into intersections of rows and columns, known as cells. Not only can data be captured, but it can also be processed for further analysis. This is facilitated in that cells can be derivates of other cells. For example, one cell can provide the total of a set of numbers in other cells. In such further processing of data, spreadsheets are incredibly versatile. They are omnipresent in industry and I assume they need very little introduction.

   In small organizations or departments, we often see both transaction processing systems *and* management information systems implemented using spreadsheets.

Database: The database provides a far more structured representation of data, and is usually to be preferred over the spreadsheet when data structures become increasingly large and more complex. Small databases are often part of office application suites, so they are inexpensive to start off with. As the transaction data grows in size, more professional database systems would be used to structure and store them. Advanced features of more professional database systems include multi-user access, authorization, backup, and so on.

Reporting package: Management information can be provided through reporting packages, which specialize in the provision of management information from databases. You can use either the built-in functionality that some databases provide or a third-party (commercial) report generator.

Integrated systems: An integrated system, often called *enterprise resource planning* system, or simply *enterprise system*, integrates the functionality of several individual software packages into one. This leads to efficiency and it avoids complex and error-prone data sharing between the individual packages. It is not without complexity though, because often these systems need substantial configuration to make them work. Integrated enterprise systems are common in larger organizations with multiple branches.

   The integrated system provides of course a substantial amount of information for managerial decision-making. There are usually links with spreadsheets too, so that the data can be subject to further processing and analysis.

Business intelligence system: *Business intelligence* systems represent the top end of management information systems. They often work on the basis of a data set from an integrated system. These systems provide integrated analysis capabilities and extended visualization of the transaction data. We also see many spreadsheet applications in this situation. Some business intelligence systems provide additional processing and preparation of data which is then exported to the spreadsheet. Other systems are more tightly integrated with spreadsheets, and use the same user interface to provide extended analysis capabilities.

1.4. **Design**

Design is one of the most overused terms in the field of information systems. So let us first have a look at what the word really means. Designing is first and foremost an exercise in *shaping*: we have a set of loose elements that we organize and arrange into a structure that is more than the sum of its parts. We call the result of this shaping exercise the 'design', and we can attribute certain characteristics to it, such as its desirability, its attractiveness, or its fitness for a particular purpose. This is true for everything that we design, whether it is a house, a sculpture, or an information system.

So what is it that we shape when we design a management information system? I would argue that we *shape data from transaction systems into management information, for the purpose of managerial decision-making.* It is this perspective on design that we will adopt in this book. We shape data through structuring, querying, aggregation, and visualization. When we look at the results of our design, we judge its suitability by the degree to which it can support managerial decision-making.

The term design is often encountered in other areas of information systems development as well. I should like to mention a few, and point out the similarities and differences between the use of the term in these areas and the view adopted in this book.

Designing solutions to problems: We can conceptualize design as part of a problem-solving cycle. This conceptualization was put forward by Herbert Simon, the 1978 Nobel Prize winner in economics. He argued that problem-solving can be broken down into three phases: intelligence, design, and choice. In the intelligence phase, you explore and analyse the problem. In the design phase, you develop a range of possible solutions to the problem. In the choice phase, you decide which of these possible solutions is the most appropriate one.

This is a very high-level conceptualization of design. Using this approach, we can view the whole development of the management information system as a possible solution for a management problem.

Designing data structures: A more narrow view of design is the analysis of data structures and the design of the data model. This is a very important exercise that takes place as part of the development of a management information system. We shall pay significant attention to the structuring of data sets for management decision-making.

Designing database queries: This perspective of design focuses on the creation of *queries*, instructions to the database as to what subset of data to retrieve from the data that is available to us. The structuring of the query is often called query design. Again this is an important part of designing information systems and we shall cover it in this book.

Designing management reports: This view of design looks very specifically at the end-product of the management information system, the management report. It involves looking at options that involve visual layouts, and whether data should be represented using tables or using charts. We shall pay significant attention to the visual design of management information as well in this book.

Designing system functionality: This is again a broader view of design, in which the designer specifies the functionality of the information system. It often encompasses data design mentioned previously. It is also known as functional design.

Designing system configurations: We have seen that management information systems can be part of different configurations. The identification of the most appropriate configuration is also called design.

It often involves more technical discussions on what system exports what data. This is usually further specified as technical design, architecture design, or infrastructure design.

You can see that there are many interpretations of the term design. In practice, it is important to be sensitive to the confusion that often arises when information systems professionals talk of designing systems. One professional may have an altogether different interpretation than the other.

1.5. **Information overload**

An important theme in the design of management information systems is that managers (and indeed most people) struggle with the processing of large sets of data. Given too much information they will quickly succumb to a state that is known as *information overload*. This is a mental state where being served with additional data becomes detrimental, not beneficial to judgement.

Herbert Simon was among the first to realize that a surplus of information should be connected to a shortage of something else. He is famous for saying: 'What information consumes is rather obvious: it consumes the attention of its recipients. Hence a wealth of information creates a poverty of attention, and a need to allocate that attention efficiently among the overabundance of information sources that might consume it' (Simon 1971). In other words: attention deficit and information overload are two sides of the same coin.

Psychologists have been making good progress in finding out the limits of our information processing capabilities. This is perhaps partly so because such a question lends itself well to laboratory experiments. In an experimental setting, researchers can present you with data, following which they can measure your response to that data (e.g. your success at recalling the data). If they present you with an increasing amount of data, they can measure the extent to which you can keep responding successfully. The idea is that after a certain amount of data, the quality of your responses will start to suffer, up to the point where more data produces no more successful responses.

The result of these and other experiments is that there seems to be an upper limit of six or seven to our information processing capabilities, irrespective of the form in which that information comes to us (Miller 1956; Pollack 1952). This limit of seven refers to the number of absolute values on one attribute that we can identify and recall in our short-term memory (Shiffrin and Nosofsky 1994).

Our limited capacity to deal with information should be an important consideration in the design of information systems. Russel Ackoff famously argued that the last thing a manager needs was *more* information: 'I do not deny that most managers lack a good deal of information that they should have. But I do deny that this is the most important informational deficiency from which they suffer. It seems to me that they suffer more from an overabundance of irrelevant information' (Ackoff 1967, p. 147). We thus need to judge the appropriateness of a management information system by the extent to which it can suppress irrelevant data.

The role of information systems in combatting information overload has been put to the test in an important set of experiments conducted by the University of Minnesota's management information systems research centre (MISRC). The *Minnesota experiments*, as they have come to be known (Dickson, Senn, and Chervany 1977), represent one of the first major advancements in research on information systems.

The experiments that this centre conducted were all based on management games: games that simulate the operations of a fictional company, and where players assume the roles of managers. At each turn of the game, the players are presented with information about the current state of affairs in the company. This could, for example, be inventory levels or sales figures for certain brands. Given this information, the players take a number of decisions, for example, which goods to purchase to replenish inventory levels, or which marketing budgets to adjust for which brand. These decisions were then incorporated in the game, and the situation for the next turn is calculated.

The researchers varied the types of reports that these groups received after each turn. At the end of the game a researcher can look at the performance of each of the groups and see which group made the most profit. You can then conclude which type of report was the most appropriate.

What did we learn from this and other research? First of all, *when a manager is provided with data, one cannot automatically assume that the data will receive attention in the first place.* A manager's span of attention is limited, and the level of interest in specific data can be highly personal. Consequently, the attention devoted to data is entirely at the manager's discretion.

Second, *the more data is provided, the more likely it is that each piece of data will get less attention.* This is simply because there will be more demand for attention, and it is therefore more likely that the 'available' attention will be spread thinly over the data. Similarly, the *less* data you provide, the *more* attention each datum is likely to get.

Finally, *the more data you provide, the more unequal the division of attention can be for each datum.* One should not automatically assume that a manager will try to distribute the attention equally over all the data that is available. This, again, is a highly personal process. Just like other people, managers exhibit a number of cognitive biases. For example, they may spend a disproportional amount of attention on the first or last piece of data supplied.

The main lesson therefore is that an information system designer should, wherever possible, ruthlessly economize on providing information. By doing so the designer ensures that (1) the likelihood increases that the manager will develop an interest and attend to the data, (2) avoid spreading the manager's attention too thinly, and (3) make it clear for the manager where to spend attention, to avoid situations where the manager randomly distributes attention all over the place.

There are two important ways to economize on the volume of transaction processing data: data *aggregation* and data *visualization*. Data aggregation provides summary statistics of underlying data. Data visualization transforms tabular data into charts. We will look at each technique in significant detail in the next chapters of this book.

1.6. **Structure of the book**

Previously I said that the design of management information systems is the shaping of data from transaction processing systems into management information for the purpose of management decision-making. There are thus two important elements to discuss: the shaping of data into

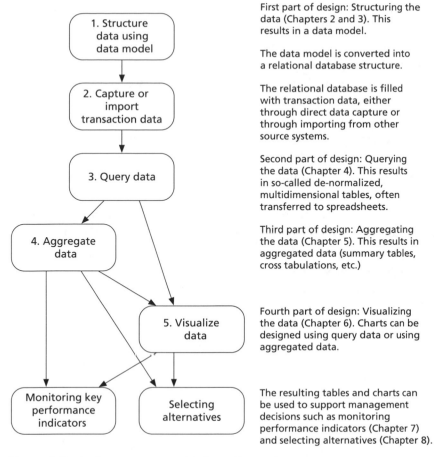

First part of design: Structuring the data (Chapters 2 and 3). This results in a data model.

The data model is converted into a relational database structure.

The relational database is filled with transaction data, either through direct data capture or through importing from other source systems.

Second part of design: Querying the data (Chapter 4). This results in so-called de-normalized, multidimensional tables, often transferred to spreadsheets.

Third part of design: Aggregating the data (Chapter 5). This results in aggregated data (summary tables, cross tabulations, etc.)

Fourth part of design: Visualizing the data (Chapter 6). Charts can be designed using query data or using aggregated data.

The resulting tables and charts can be used to support management decisions such as monitoring performance indicators (Chapter 7) and selecting alternatives (Chapter 8).

Figure 4 Designing management information systems

management information and their role in management decision-making. The book is organized accordingly into two parts.

Figure 4 presents a graphical overview of the structure of the book. The figure also represents a typical process flow of the design of a management information system. You would start with *data structuring* (step 1), and develop what is called a *data model*. The data model will form the foundation for the database of the management information system.

When the data model is finished and the database has been created, the database would need to be filled ('populated' is the technical term) with transactional data (step 2). Depending on the scope and size of the data, this can be done either through direct data capture or through interfaces from source systems. As we have seen previously, this is not necessarily a straightforward process.

When the transaction data is in the system, we can start *querying* that data in a variety of ways (step 3). Querying results in so-called de-normalized, multi-dimensional tables. The meaning of these terms will become clear later in the book, but for now it is sufficient to know that these tables are essentially 'projections' of the underlying data. Such tables are frequently imported into spreadsheets where they can be made subject to further analysis.

The tables that are the result of the querying process are often very large, and studying them will raise the possibility of information overload. We thus need to proceed to the next steps of designing management informa-tion systems, which involve *aggregating* (step 4) and *visualizing* the data (step 5). These two skills, as we have seen earlier, are aimed at overcoming information overload associated with large volumes of data. Aggregating the data results in the tables and visualizing the data results in the charts that are so common in management information reporting.

The book closely follows these five steps. Here is a brief overview of the chapters of Part I:

Structuring data, part 1: This chapter discusses the basics of structuring data sets. This allows us to understand the structure of data sets from transaction processing systems, and to develop the structure for management information systems.

Structuring data, part 2: This chapter discusses some more advanced concepts of structuring data sets, including inheritance and entity life cycles.

Querying data: This chapter discusses the retrieval of data from data sets. It focuses on the design of queries to retrieve data from the data structures.

Aggregating data: This chapter as well as the next one focus on the two ways of reducing information overload in management information systems. The first technique is aggregation.

Visualizing data: This chapter discusses the ways that management data sets can be visualized.

The second part of the book deals with two specific management decisions, and how the design of information systems can be judged by the extent to which they support these decisions. Here is a brief overview of them:

Monitoring key figures: An important task of a manager is to examine key figures and to monitor whether anything unusual is happening and whether everything is going according to plan. This chapter looks at this particular type of decision and covers the support of management information systems in more detail.

Selecting alternatives: Another important task of a manager is to select one alternative out of many. For example, the manager may need to select a suitable candidate for a job vacancy out of a range of applicants. Or the manager may need to select a suitable vendor to procure a specific commodity product. This chapter looks at this task in more detail and suggests ways in which management information systems may help.

1.7. **Case description**

This book uses a simple case situation for which we will build, step-by-step, a management information system. I have opted for a fictitious sales department, assumed to be located in a medium-sized company. We shall assume further that we will be managing that department, and we will design a management information system to manage this department effectively.

We can keep most of the additional description of this case fairly abstract. We need to assume that the sales department is organized into three sales teams, called Alpha, Beta, and Gamma. A customer can buy certain products from your company, which include (in no particular order): wine, oranges, soap, apples, and candles. Orders are usually fairly large and so your sales agents usually have appointments with customers first. During these appointments, the sales agents discuss possible orders with the customers.

Obviously, in terms of sales management, you are interested in the volume of sales, as well as the revenue it generates. The management information system should provide these figures and break them down according to customer, according to product, and according to sales team. We shall use these requirements in the next parts of this book to design a suitable management information system.

⬜ FURTHER READING

A number of introductory texts on management information systems are available. Popular ones include texts by Laudon and Laudon (2004), O'Brien and Marakas (2006), and Haag et al. (2007).

This book assumes that you will have a basic working knowledge on the operations of spreadsheets and small databases. If you want to brush up on these skills, it is useful simply to gain access to an office spreadsheet or a small database and start experimenting with the available options. There are, of course, many books available that can help you, most of which are tied to specific commercial products.

If you want to read more about information overload, I recommend articles by Kahneman (1973), Simon (1974), and Norman and Bobrow (1975). These articles discuss a set of mental processes that are collectively called *attention management*. Further in-depth discussion on the management of attention can be found in Allport (1980) and Styles (2006).

Part I

Designing Information Systems

2 Structuring data, part 1

KEY THEMES

When you have read this chapter, you should be able to define those key concepts in your own words, and you should also be able to:

1. Model the entities of the managerial domain.
2. Model the relationships that exist between these entities and identify the types of relationships.
3. Factor out categorical attribute types and many to many relationships.
4. Transfer the entities and relationships into R-table structures.

2.1. Introduction

In any managerial situation we can assume that there is some understanding of what it is that needs to be managed: employees, budgets, customers, production processes, and so on. We would say that these are the *entities* of our particular management domain. When we design information systems to support the management of these entities, we must first seek to obtain a more precise understanding of them. The techniques that allow us to do so are the focus of this chapter and the next.

We model the structures of data using conceptual diagrams. The complete set of diagrams describing the entities from our managerial domain represents our *data model*. The data model can be drawn using a variety of diagramming techniques.

In industry there are a number of techniques around. I will introduce you to a popular one in this chapter: the Entity–Relationship diagramming technique. The *Entity–Relationship diagram* (or ER diagram), introduced by Chen in 1976, was one of the first techniques to graphically represent entities. In its original form it continues to be widely used, even though a number of techniques have been developed that extend or replace it.

My strategy for exposing you to ER diagrams is to first explain how entities are modelled and how you convert those into so-called R-tables. Following on from that I will discuss entity relationships, and point at several complications that often occur when you model those.

This chapter is the first part of the data structuring material in this book. The next chapter will cover the UML class diagrams, which extend ER diagrams, and it will cover the structuring of some special cases of which you should be aware.

2.2. **Entities**

A data model contains two important ingredients: entities and relationships. The *entity* is the first ingredient. It is defined as a 'thing' which can be distinctly identified (Chen 1976, p. 10). Examples from our case include Sales Team, Sales Agent, Customer, Sales Order, and so on.

It is important to make a distinction between abstract concepts and concrete examples of abstract concepts. For example, two fictional people called Joe and Mary can be concrete examples of the abstract concept Sales Agent. You will remember we had three sales teams called Alpha, Beta, and Gamma. These three sales teams are concrete examples of the abstract concept Sales Team. When we structure data, we should be looking for the abstract concepts only. They provide the containers for the concrete examples, and they will provide the structures that will allow us to store the examples.

The label for an abstract concept was originally the *entity set* (Chen 1976), but it has become common to talk of the abstract concept as the entity, and of the concrete examples as the *instances* of the entity. That is the convention that we will use in this book. So, we would talk about the entity Sales Agent, of which Joe and Mary are instances.

Figure 1 Entities

Identifying entities is not, on the whole, a clear-cut exercise. In your managerial domain, you will encounter many concrete instances. When you attempt to model those, you need to shift from the concrete instances to the more abstract concepts. In that process you often have a number of choices. Take Joe for example. He could be representing the entity Sales Agent, but also the entity Person, Customer, and so on. These examples are not even mutually exclusive: Joe could happily represent all these and more. You should look very carefully at your managerial domain to guide you in the selection of the appropriate entities.

In your Entity–Relationship diagram you would draw the entity as a rectangular box with the name of the entity in the box. Figure 1 gives an example of five entities that we might encounter in our case study.

I need to draw your attention to a number of features of the ER diagram in Figure 1. First, the position of the entities on the diagram is arbitrary. The fact that the entity Sales Team is at the top left, and the entity Customer at the very right does not carry any meaning. Also, it is a convention to put the name of the entity in singular form. So, even though we are modelling multiple sales teams, we would still call the entity Sales Team. In terms of format, entity names are written with a capital letter, and in bold typeface. This is the standard format in which computer packages draw them. These conventions are useful to distinguish them from attributes, discussed in the next section.

Databases store instances of entities in special kinds of tables called R-tables. The *relational table* or *R-table* was first introduced by Codd in 1974. It is also known as the *relation*, but since I will also use the term relation in the context of ER diagrams, I shall use the older term R-table to avoid confusion. Many popular database systems today are *relational databases*, that is, built around R-table structures.

We shall look at R-tables in more detail shortly but for now it is important to remember that *every entity in our model is going to correspond to exactly one R-table*. The R-table has the same name as the entity with which it corresponds, but there are two naming conventions that you need to watch out for. First, by convention, the name of the R-table is always in lowercase letters. Second, spaces in names are not normally allowed and you are encouraged to replace those with the underscore character (_). For example, the names of the corresponding R-tables of the entities from Figure 1 are `sales_team`, `sales_agent`, `sales_order`, `customer`, and `product`. These conventions may sound somewhat arbitrary at the moment but the reason for them will become clear in Chapter 4.

2.3. **Attributes**

Having identified the entities we can now proceed to identify the characteristics of the entities. These characteristics are commonly known as attributes. An *attribute* is a property of an entity, a distinctly identifiable characteristic that all instances can have. For example, we can identify an attribute Name for the entity Sales Agent. All sales agents have a name, or in other words, all sales agents have the property Name. For the entity Product, we can identify the attribute Price.

Attributes have *values*. The value is a specification of the attribute for a particular entity. When an instance has no value for a particular attribute, we would call this a *missing value*, or, more technically, a NULL value.

Attributes in an ER diagram can be represented using the so-called circle notation. Each circle corresponds to exactly one attribute. Figure 2 displays two examples.

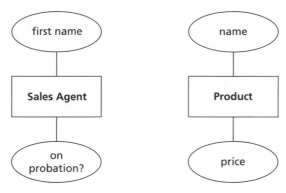

Figure 2 Attributes

As a convention the name of the attribute does not start with a capital letter. This serves as an extra visual cue to set attributes apart from entities. You can see that the circle representation has the drawback that it takes up a lot of space. It can only really be used with a very small number of attributes. In the next chapter, we will discuss a better notation.

Having discussed attributes, we are now in a position to examine the structure of an R-table somewhat further. An example of an R-table for the entity Product is provided below.

```
product_id name    price
========== ======  =====
1          Orange  1
2          Soap    5
3          Wine    10
4          Apple   1
5          Candle  7
```

An example of an R-table for the entity Sales Agent is provided below.

```
agent_id name on_probation
======== ==== ============
1        Jim  true
2        Tom  true
3        Mary false
4        Jim  false
5        Jack false
```

You can see that an R-table looks a bit like any old table but there are a few rules that an R-table must adhere to that a normal table does not. These rules are:

Columns: The columns should represent the attributes of the entity. They have a column name which identifies that column in the R-table. The name of the column must be unique. There is no order preference in the columns. In the product table for example, I could have put the column price in front of name and it would have represented the same R-table.

Rows: The rows should represent an instance of the entity, with one row corresponding to exactly one entity. Rows do not have a name in the same way that columns do. There is no order preference in the rows either. For example, if I had placed Wine (row 3) on the first row (where Orange is), it would have been the same R-table. I have sorted the rows according to the column product_id, but that is an arbitrary choice; I could also have sorted them according to their name, for example.

Row duplication: There can be no duplication of rows. Each row represents exactly one instance. For example, if I had left out the column product_id, and added another row with name Orange and price 1, that would be a duplicate of the first row. An R-table would not allow this because it would not be able to tell whether these two rows represent one single instance, or whether there are actually two products that happen to have the same attribute values.

Primary keys: To avoid row duplication to occur accidently, it is common to introduce an extra column, the so-called ID column, which gives each row a unique identity. It is normally a number that increases whenever a new row is introduced. Such a column that gives a row a unique identity is called a *primary key*. Primary keys are never NULL. We do not display them in ER diagrams, they are a feature of R-tables only.

The naming of the columns in the R-tables follows the same convention as the naming for the R-tables that we discussed earlier. Each column represents exactly one attribute name. They are by convention always lower case and do not contain spaces. The reasons for this will become clear in Chapter 4.

2.4. **Attribute types**

Thus far we have not really said anything in detail about the attributes themselves. Yet it is clear that an attribute Price is different from an attribute Name. How is it different? The main difference is in the range of allowable values. For Price, we would say only numbers are allowed, and for Name this would be strings of letters. It is good practice to specify precisely what the allowable range of data values is going to be. We do so by specifying the *attribute type*. Synonyms sometimes encountered for attribute type are the *value range* or *data type*.

A list of attribute types is provided below.

Number: Any numeric value. If necessary, the values can be further specified into integer and real numbers. An example would be the quantity of a product sold, or the price of a product.

Text: Free text, not predefined. In a more technical environment, this is usually called a *string*, or *varchar* (for 'variable characters'). An example would be the name of a sales agent or the name of a product.

Category: Predefined, non-numeric values. Ranking of the values is sometimes possible, sometimes not. Examples include attributes such as Product Type, with the predefined values Food and Non-Food, or Sales Team, with the predefined values Alpha, Beta, and Gamma.

I need to issue an immediate warning here. Take a note if you encounter an attribute that you believe is of type Category. At a later stage in the structuring process, you will get rid of the Category attribute by converting the category into an entity and introducing a so-called one-to-many relationship. The procedure for this will be described in more detail later in this chapter.

True/False: An attribute that is modelled as a True/False question. The response is either True or False or Yes or No. To identify an attribute of this type, the name of the attribute is usually worded as a question too, for example: Is Cancelled?

A special attribute type is the *time stamp*, which is a date or time that a specific event occurs. The event is the attribute and the time stamp is the value. For example, a sales order is created on a specific date, a production order is started on a specific date, goods are despatched on a specific date, and so on. Many management information systems need those time stamps for analysis. For example, using these time stamps we can see how the total volume of sales generated this year compares to the volume of sales generated last year. It is therefore very important to be precise about the specific time stamp that we are recording. Here are the most common ones.

Day of Week: Monday, Tuesday, Wednesday, Thursday, Friday, Saturday, and Sunday. Represented with these categorical values, or occasionally as number. I recommend formatting as a categorical variable exclusively so as not to confuse this type with Day of Month.

Day of Month: Ranging from 1 to 28, 29, 30, or 31 depending on the month. Represented as number.

Week: Ranging from 1 to 52 or occasionally 53 depending on the year. Represented as a number, week 1 being the first week of the year.

Month: Ranging from 1 to 12. Represented both as number and as Category (January, February).

Year: The year according to the Gregorian calendar.

Time: Representing a specific time during the day. For example, 06:00. Sometimes seconds and milliseconds are added if more precision is needed, for example, 06:00.01.

Date: Combination of Day of month, Month, and Year

Time stamp: A combination of Date and Time.

For time stamps it is important to realize that there is a distinction between the attribute type and the attribute format. The *attribute format* is the way an attribute value is represented to a user. It does not say anything about how that attribute value is stored in our system. An example is the format of a date. In the United States, a date is normally formatted as MM/DD/YYYY. In Europe, a date is normally formatted as DD/MM/YYYY. The format is flexible in that a user can change it in a whim, without changing the underlying value in the database.

The distinction between attribute type and attribute format begins to blur when the attribute format performs numeric or categorical conversions. For example, we can record the date as a 'Date', but the format can represent just the week number for that date, and so when we see the attribute, it is as if that date has the type Week. Similarly, a format can start to convert two categorical values such as 'Strongly Agree' and 'Slightly

Agree' into one value 'Agree'. In these situations, it is recommendable to specify the most precise attribute type that is available, so that we can transform it into more imprecise formats as we retrieve the data.

2.5. **Relationships**

Entities are an important ingredient of any model but they do not exist in isolation. Often we are not so much interested in the entities themselves, but rather in the relationships between them. For example, I may be keen to manage sales agents and to manage sales teams, but to manage both effectively, I will need to know which sales agents are connected to which sales teams. This *relationship*, the one that links sales agents and sales teams together, will therefore need to be modelled as well.

The ER diagram models such a relationship with a straight line connecting two entities. We often, but not always, give the relationship a name too, for better understanding. This name is either put into a diamond shape in the middle or put close to the line. Figure 3 associates the Sales Agent with the Sales Team in this way.

Relationship lines can have more features to give some more detail of the type of relationship. Without any feature, that is, a straight line as depicted in Figure 3, it means that the relationship always associates one instance of one entity with one instance of another entity. Thus, Figure 3 expresses the relationship between a sales team and a sales agent, and specifically this: that one sales team is always associated with one sales agent, and the other way around. We would say that this is a *one-to-one relationship*.

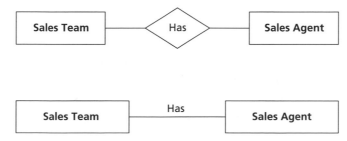

Figure 3 Relationships

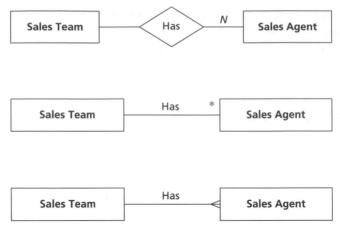

Figure 4 One to many relationships

Obviously this type of relationship is not the one that is correct in our case study. One sales team can have *many* sales agents, even though one sales agent is only part of one sales team. We would thus say the relationship between sales team and sales agent is *one-to-many*.

We model a one-to-many relationship by giving the ends of the connecting line an adornment. This can be done in three ways. The ER diagram would place an N at the 'many' end of the relationship line. This is the original notation. A new notation is to put an asterisk (*) at the 'many' end, as is the convention for the UML class diagrams discussed in the next chapter. Besides the N and the asterisk you will also often encounter a so-called crow's-foot at the end of the connecting line. This notation was introduced by Barker (1989). I personally prefer this notation over the others because it depicts the multiplicity of the relationship so elegantly. You can judge for yourself in Figure 4.

We have seen how the crow-foot notation was used to depict the 'many'-end of a relationship. The absence of a crow-foot in turn was to indicate the 'one'-end of the relationship. We now shall discuss two additional endings for these types of relationships.

These two endings are the circle (or ring) and the dash. The circle is representing 'zero' and the dash is representing 'exactly one'. We use the circle and the dash to say something about the optionality of the relationship.

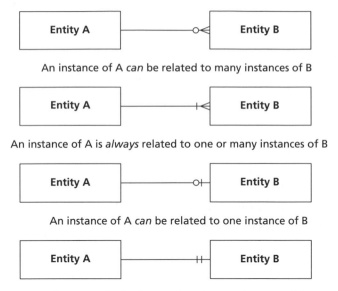

An instance of A *can* be related to many instances of B

An instance of A is *always* related to one or many instances of B

An instance of A *can* be related to one instance of B

An instance of A is *always* related to one instance of B

Figure 5 Extra endings for ER relationships

The circle is meant to indicate that a zero relationship is allowed. Let us take for example the sales team and sales agent relationship. If it is possible for a sales team to *not* have sales agents, we would add a circle to the sales agent end of the relationship. If it is possible for a sales agent to *not* be part of a sales team, we would add a circle to the sales team end of the relationship.

The dash would be used to indicate that the relationship is *not* optional but mandatory. We would specify the dash if a sales agent always had to be part of a sales team, or if a sales team would always have to contain at least one sales agent.

Instead of circles and dashes, the relationship is sometimes drawn as a dotted line to indicate optionality (e.g. Barker 1989). Figure 5 depicts the four possible types of endings, as well as corresponding examples of how to 'read out loud' the relationship as it is described.

The optionality of the relationship has implications for the foreign keys. If a relationship is optional, it is permissible for a foreign key to have a NULL value. For example, the sales agent table has a foreign key to denote the sales team, but if the sales agent in question does not belong to a sales agent, then that foreign key value can be NULL. Likewise, if a relationship is not optional, a foreign key cannot have a NULL value.

How do we convert a relationship to an R-table? We cannot just use two R-tables, one for sales teams and one for sales agents, because that does not give us information about the relationship between sales teams and sales agents. The solution is to add a pointer to the R-table which represents the entity at the 'many' end of the relationship. Such a pointer is called the *Foreign Key* (or FK). The foreign key should refer back to the entity at the 'one' end. It thus represents the primary key of the other entity. You can see below how the two R-tables are constructed. Each table has a primary key, and the entity at the many end (the sales agent) has a foreign key that points to the entity at the one end (the sales team).

```
team_id name
======= ======
1       Alpha
2       Beta
3       Gamma
```

```
agent_id name on_probation team_id
======== ==== ============ =======
1        Jim  true         1
2        Tom  true         2
3        Mary false        1
4        Jim  false        2
5        Jack false        NULL
```

This table links Jim No. 1 and Mary to sales team Alpha, and Tom and Jim No. 2 to sales team Beta. Note that Gamma does not have any sales agents linked to it, and that Jack is not part of a sales team (its foreign key is NULL). A foreign key can be NULL but you can also expressly prohibit this in most available database systems.

Figure 6 shows a more elaborate Entity–Relationship model for our case study. You will see that there are two so-called many-to-many relationships in Figure 6. I shall discuss these somewhat more in the next chapter. You will also note that one of the relationship descriptions has an arrow pointing to the left (<), which indicates that the description should be read 'from right to left'. In this example, you need to read 'one sales order consists of many products'.

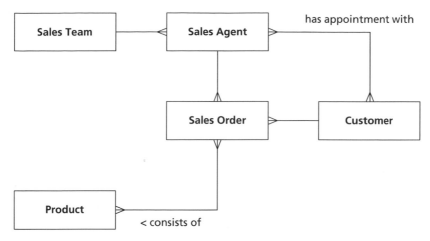

Figure 6 ER diagram with one-to-many relationships

I spoke earlier about attributes with a type Category. If an attribute type is categorical, then the most appropriate way to model the attribute is to create an entity (representing the category), and to create a one-to-many relationship from the categorical entity to the entity.

For the entity Product example, we may have an attribute called Product Type, with the predefined values Food and Non-Food. The most appropriate way to model this is to define a special entity called Product Type, with an attribute called Name (attribute type Text). Each product type entity would have a primary key that can function as a foreign key to be used in product.

A similar example is the one with customers and their customer status. Let us assume that a customer proceeds along the following statuses: they start out as leads, they can then become prospects, and they finally become 'paying' customers proper. There are thus three status values: lead, prospect, and customer: a classic example of a categorical value, and one that should be ironed out with a special Status entity.

There are two advantages of getting rid of categorical values this way. The first is that it allows us to examine the categories on their own, and modify them as we see fit. For example, if we want to introduce another customer status, we only have to add one additional instance. Second, it allows us to introduce extra attributes for the category, which can often be useful.

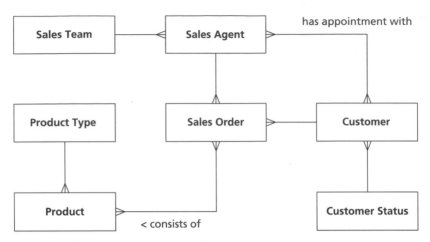

Figure 7 ER diagram with categorical entities

Figure 7 shows our Entity–Relationship diagram with the two categorical entities previously discussed.

A frequent error that students make when they start drawing relationships is to include redundant one-to-many relationships. Figure 8 shows an example. You will see that in this example, one sales team can have more than one sales agent, and one sales agent can have more than one sales order. Now many students think they have to include an additional one-to-many relationship between sales team and sales order, thereby bypassing the sales agent. After all, a sales team can have more than one sales order too. Can you identify whether this relationship needs to be there?

The relationship should not be there because it introduces *redundancy*. Redundancy implies that we will allow the same data to be entered multiple times (in this case twice). Redundancy is bad because along with it, through the back door, comes the possibility of *data corruption*. Corruption occurs when we change the data in one part of the system, but forget to change it in another part of the system. To prevent this from happening in the first place, data redundancy should be avoided whenever you can.

In the example of Figure 8, the two original one-to-many relationships already 'connect' a sales team with a sales order: through the sales agent. If we want to know which sales team is associated with which sales order, we would proceed as follows: First, in the R-table `sales_order`, look up the foreign key for sales agent. Using the foreign key for sales agent, locate that

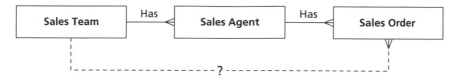

Figure 8 An extra relationship?

sales agent in the R-table `sales_agent`. Look there for the foreign key for sales team. Using that foreign key, find the sales team.

Had we introduced a foreign key for sales team in the R-table `sales_order` (by introducing the redundant relationship) we are introducing the possibility of data corruption. On the one hand, we can link a sales order to sales team using the direct link. On the other hand, we can link a sales order to sales team using the indirect link (via the sales agent). If both links represent the same relationship, then it is possible that we corrupt the data by entering one correct link indirectly and another incorrect one directly. Such possibilities for data corruption are the causes of many frustrations in organizations.

2.6. **Many-to-many relationships**

A *many-to-many relationship* occurs when we have two one-to-many relationship for two entities in either direction. We have already seen two many-to-many relationships in Figure 6.

It is important to understand that a many-to-many relationship is simply a case of two overlapping one-to-many relationships. So, rather than interpreting a many-to-many relationship as: 'many sales agents can have appointments with many customers', it is better to interpret it as follows: 'one sales agent can have an appointment with many customers', and 'one customer can have an appointment with many sales agents'. Similarly, the many-to-many relationship between product and sales order should be read as follows: 'one sales order consists of many products', and 'one product can be a part of many sales orders'.

Just like you should remove categorical attribute types by creating new categorical entities, you should remove many-to-many relationships by

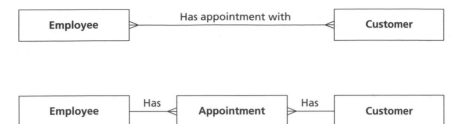

Figure 9 An entity to replace a many-to-many relationship

creating new auxiliary entities. The auxiliary entity should connect the two original entities using two one-to-many relationships.

Take our example of sales agents and customers. The top row of Figure 9 gives the example. The bottom row provides the intermediary entity, which we will call Appointment. The additional benefit is that we can now store some additional attributes together with the appointment, such as the time stamp, and whether it was cancelled or not.

The other many-to-many relationship in the example was between sales order and product. We can remove this relationship by introducing an intermediary entity that we could call Line Item. One sales order can have many line items. One product can be part of many line items. A line item is always connected to one order and one product.

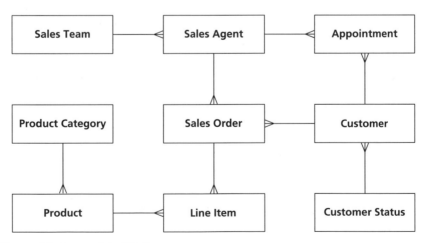

Figure 10 A complete ER diagram

The reason why you need to transform many-to-many relationships into auxiliary entities is because this will facilitate the transfer of the diagrams into R-tables. We will have to introduce an auxiliary R-table to link entities that have many-to-many relationships. Of course the auxiliary R-table would have its own primary key, but it would have foreign keys to the entities that it connects.

Here is an example of what the `line_item` R-table would look like:

```
item_id order_id product_id quantity
======= ======== ========== ========
1       1        1          6
2       1        5          34
3       2        3          24
. . .   . . .    . . .      . . .
```

Can you trace back what data is stored here? We have two sales orders. The first sales order consists of 6 oranges and 34 candles. The second sales order consists of 24 bottles of wine.

I should note that disposing many-to-many relationships at the diagram level is not conventional practice. Indeed no database textbook that I am aware of argues that diagrams should rule out many-to-many relationships. Instead they would advise the creation of an auxiliary R-table as soon as the diagram is converted into R-tables. I have found it easier to upgrade that auxiliary table to an 'auxiliary entity' straightaway, so that the one-to-one mapping from entity to R-table is preserved, and one does not end up with more R-tables than entities.

Figure 10 provides the complete Entity–Relationship diagram that we have developed so far, with the categorical and the auxiliary entities.

Appendix 1 provides the structure of the corresponding R-tables, and also provides examples of data that can be captured using the structure.

▢ FURTHER READING

In this chapter I have covered the basics of Entity–Relationship diagrams, as well as the R-table structure that underlies the diagrams. You should now be able to 'read' existing ER diagrams, for example, those that describe data from transaction processing systems. You should now also be able to create your own diagrams, for example, to identify the most important concepts in the managerial domain and their relationships.

A range of text books on database design is available that cover the concepts from this chapter in more detail. Popular ones include Date (2000) and Kendall and Kendall (1999).

The R-tables and the associated relational structure of databases were first introduced by Codd (1970). The ER diagrams were first introduced by Chen (1976). An ER textbook that introduces the crow-feet notation is Barker (1989).

3 Structuring data, part 2

KEY CONCEPTS

UML	Inheritance
Object	State
Association	Transition
Generalization	

KEY THEMES

When you have read this chapter, you should be able to define those key concepts in your own words, and you should also be able to:

1. Identify the differences between Entity–Relationship diagrams and UML diagrams.
2. Model a hierarchy of entities through generalization.
3. Model the lifecycle of an entity using states and transitions.
4. Transfer hierarchies and entity lifecycle stages to R-table structures.

3.1. Introduction

In the previous chapter we discussed the fundamentals of structuring data. In this chapter we will be building on this material and discuss an important alternative to ER diagrams, UML class diagrams.

The Unified Modeling Language or UML is a diagramming language that, among other things, recasts entities into classes. The fundamental notions of entities and classes are very similar, but the terminology is slightly different. I will discuss the UML concepts in a bit more detail in this chapter, because you will frequently encounter class diagrams instead of ER diagrams.

A class diagram is in many ways an 'upgrade' of the ER diagram. For example, it provides an elegant conceptual drawing technique which is known as *generalization*. This is a way to capture hierarchical data into an

ER diagram. We will look at this concept some more in this chapter and provide a few examples.

In addition we shall look at a new type of diagram called State Transition Diagrams. These diagrams represent the lifecycle of an entity. They are important for management information systems because we are often interested in the different stages that the entities of our managerial domain pass through. State Transition Diagrams allow us to model these stages.

The reason why we are looking at these modelling techniques is because we need to be aware of all the key tools with which we can structure data. When our database structure is ready and implemented, we can fill the database with data from the transaction systems. When the data is there, we can start querying the database. The techniques for querying data will be discussed in the next chapter.

3.2. **UML**

The origins of UML can be traced back to the rise of a movement in software engineering called *object orientation*. At the risk of oversimplifying, object orientation is an approach in software development that advocates the integration of data and functionality into small software compartments called objects. This is in contrast to the more traditional approach in which data is separated from functionality. Object orientation has benefits, one of which is the benefit of damage containment: when a software error occurs, it is easier to isolate the error and contain the damage.

The object orientation movement spawned a great deal of new diagramming techniques, which unfortunately were not altogether compatible with each other. For example, one technique would model the object with a rectangle (as the ER diagrams did), and another would model it with a circle. This led to a rather confusing situation. As some languages became increasingly popular, advocates became increasingly outspoken about the superiority of their techniques. Those years are now often described as the 'modelling wars' (Fowler 2004).

To resolve this situation, a number of harmonization and standardization efforts took place. These were by and large unsuccessful until three proponents of popular object-oriented diagramming techniques began to merge theirs. They were Grady Booch (of the Booch method, 1993), James Rumbaugh (of the OMT method, 1991), and Ivar Jacobsen (of the OOSE method, 1992). They called their new, unified, modelling language: the *Unified Modeling Language* or *UML*.

The UML was put in the custody of a not-for-profit organization called the *Object Management Group* (OMG). It continues to be revised and extended there. In this chapter I will discuss two diagrams that are part of UML, the class diagram and the state transition diagram.

3.3. **Objects and associations**

The class diagram is an alternative version of the ER diagram, and the Unified Modeling Language uses somewhat different terminology for entities and relationships. The object-oriented version of the entity is the *class*. A class can contain several *objects*, and so an object can be compared to an instance of an entity. An object is defined as a 'discrete entity with identity, state, and behaviour' (Rumbaugh, Booch, and Jacobson 1999, p. 43). The term relationship has been replaced by the term *association*.

Despite these differences in terminology, the class diagram has a number of similarities with the ER diagram. The representation of a class is exactly the same as in an ER diagram, that is, a rectangle. The representation of an association is also exactly the same as in an ER diagram, that is, a straight line connecting the rectangles.

Attributes in a class diagram are represented by splitting the class rectangle into two, and adding the attributes as a list under the original class name. Attribute types can be included in class diagrams as well. To do so you need to put a colon behind the attribute name and then specify the attribute type as per the list of the previous chapter on page 25. Figure 1 gives an example of classes with attributes and attribute types.

You can see that, for representing attributes, the class diagram is much more efficient than the ER diagram: it would be straightforward to add another 10 attributes to a class diagram, but it would be cumbersome to add another 10 attributes to an ER diagram.

The class diagram uses a minimum and a maximum number to denote whether an association is one-to-one or one-to-many. At the end of the

Sales Agent	Product
first name: Text	name: Text
on probation? Yes/No	price: Number

Figure 1 Classes with attributes and attribute types

relationship you would put down *minimum number..maximum number*. A star (*) indicates 'Many' or 'Unlimited'. Figure 2 gives an example of association endings that are analogous with Figure 5 of Chapter 2.

There are some shortcuts as well: if an association uses just a star, that is equivalent to 0..*, and if an ending uses just 1, that is equivalent to 1..1. The absence of numbers is equivalent to 1..1 or 0..1.

One element that a class diagram has over and above an ER diagram is the *method*. A method is a description of certain behaviour that the entity can perform. For example, a Sales Agent object can create a sales order. The behaviour 'create sales order' would be a method. In object-oriented systems, different objects interact with each other by calling each other's methods. Objects are thus *active* agents, whereas entities are *passive*.

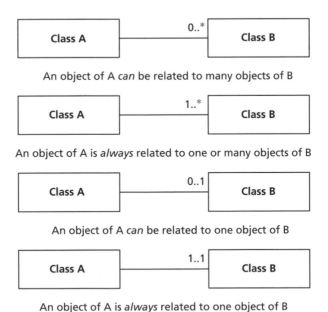

An object of A *can* be related to many objects of B

An object of A is *always* related to one or many objects of B

An object of A *can* be related to one object of B

An object of A is *always* related to one object of B

Figure 2 Extra endings for associations

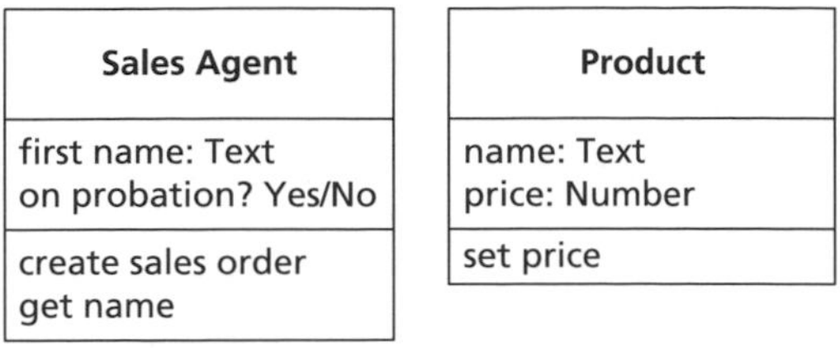

Sales Agent
first name: Text on probation? Yes/No
create sales order get name

Product
name: Text price: Number
set price

Figure 3 Classes with methods

Methods are displayed by adding another box to the class. Figure 3 gives an example.

We have already seen that management information systems are data-intensive systems, and for this reason I will not discuss the use of methods further. For data-intensive systems, you will often see methods excluded from class diagrams in practice. In that case the third box of the classes will either be empty or removed altogether.

The mapping of the class diagrams to R-tables follows the same procedures as described in the previous chapter.

3.4. **Generalizations**

Often we come across entities that we would like to model quite distinctly, but they do share common attributes with each other. For example, it is conceivable that we would like to model two types of employees: those working in the sales departments (sales agents), and those working in other departments such as accounting. Both types of employees have names and probationary arrangements and so on. But we may want to have distinctive attributes for each of the types, attributes that are not shared by the other type. For example, sales agents may have sales targets and office workers may not.

The class diagram allows us to model exactly this using a diagramming technique called *generalization*. The idea is to arrange classes into a tree, putting the more general class at the top, and the more specific classes at the bottom. You would put a triangle in the middle to make it even more explicit that you are modelling a generalization relationship. Figure 4 provides an example.

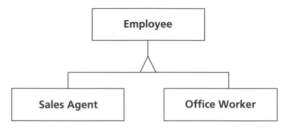

Figure 4 Generalization

The more specific class is often called the *subclass* or *child* class, and the more generic class is often called the *superclass* or *parent class*. The generalization relationship is also called an *is a* relationship. You know you have modelled generalization correctly if it makes sense to say that every subclass *is a* special kind of its superclass. For example, a sales agent *is a* special kind of employee, and an office worker also *is a* special kind of employee.

Modelling a generalization allows us to specify which attributes belong to the more general class, and which attributes are solely reserved for the special class. Figure 5 gives an example. We would say the subclass *inherits* the attributes of the superclass, and so they do not need to be modelled twice.

There are some interesting complications surrounding the generalization relationship. One is the issue of *multiple inheritance*. There is in principle no objection for a subclass to have more than one superclass.

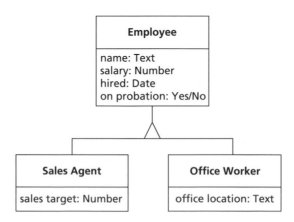

Figure 5 Attribute inheritance

It would simply inherit the attributes from both parents, a phenomenon called multiple inheritance. Problems, however, start to occur when the attributes are contradicting each other: for example, one parent may define attribute X as a number, and the other parent may define another attribute called X as text. There is no way of knowing which one should take priority. Such problems are difficult to circumvent except to simply disallow the possibility of multiple inheritance and try to model the classes in such a way that there is only one parent for each child.

3.5. **State transitions**

Often we are not so much interested in the entities themselves, or in the relationships between the entities, but in the *life cycle* of the entity. For example, in many companies a customer proceeds through different stages: they start out as leads, they can then become prospects, and they finally become customers. A sales manager would obviously be interested in the state transitions, that is, how many leads the company can convert into prospects, and how many prospects the company can convert into customers.

An ER or class diagram does not explicitly take into account that the attribute values of entities may change over time. Indeed, entities may change into other entities over time. We would say that the entity has several states, and that the states have transitions. Such states and transitions can be represented by State Transition Diagrams. Like class diagrams they are a part of the Unified Modeling Language, but they have been in existence long before they were adopted by UML. Figure 6 gives an example.

Figure 6 models how a contact can turn into a customer. The arrows describe the only state transitions that are allowed. In this example, it is not allowed for a lead to turn into a prospect without becoming a promising lead first. That is because there is no transition between promising lead and customer. Also note the circles representing start and finish: these represent where a customer starts out as (i.e. the contact), and where a customer finally ends up.

State transition diagrams are complementary to ER and class diagrams, in that they give information about the dynamic behaviour of the class.

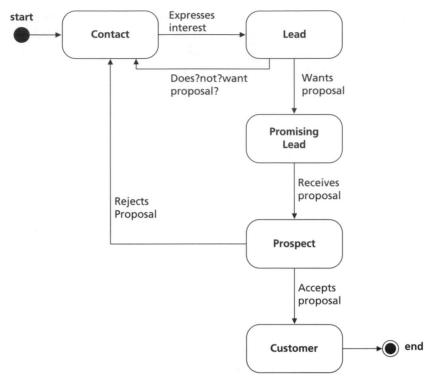

Figure 6 A state transition diagram for the class Customer

They can be used to express in greater detail the different states that a class can pass through. It is of course possible that an entity does not go through any stages at all, in which case the creation of a state transition diagram is not necessary.

Just like the ER and class diagrams, state transition diagrams exist outside the database structures. We would need to convert them into R-tables

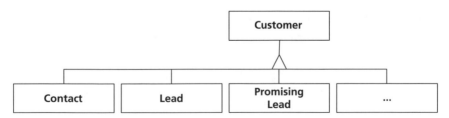

Figure 7 Objectifying states

if we want to preserve the entity lifecycle into our database. We can do this in two ways. The first way is to do it via a Status entity connected to the main entity. We have seen this at work in the previous chapter, where we factored out an R-table `customer_status` that had an attribute name with values such 'Contact', 'Lead', and so on.

The other way to do it is through generalization. In that case we would 'objectify' the state and create a separate class for the object when it is in that state. Each of these classes would be a subclass of the general class. So, you would have classes called Contact, Lead, and Promising Lead for example, which could all be subclasses of the more general class 'Customer'. Figure 7 provides an example. You need to objectify the states if the life cycle of the entity is of great importance in your managerial domain, or if each of the states is distinctively different from each other.

There is also a special vehicle in UML called the 'class-in-state' that would allow you to do something similar: for example you would model the promising lead as a class called Customer: Promising Lead. The class-in-state is not very widely used but it does allow you to create separate classes for each of the states.

□ FURTHER READING

In this chapter I have covered the UML version of ER diagrams, and I have also discussed a few special cases, generalization, and entity lifecycle diagrams. By applying these more advanced techniques, we are able to provide a rich structure of relational tables, that will in turn form the basis for our management information system.

A range of books are available to study UML in more detail. I will only mention three here. A short manual is written by Fowler (2004). The user guide is written by Booch et al. (1999), and the reference manual is written by Rumbaugh et al. (1999). Be aware that these books assume that you have a computing background and they will adopt a rather technical perspective.

We have finished the material that will allow us to structure data, and by now you should be able to design a data model that will be used for your management information system. The next step, as identified in the introduction chapter, is to ensure that the data is captured into the data structures. We can then move on to instruct the database to retrieve the data. The techniques for doing so are covered in the next chapter.

4 Querying data

KEY CONCEPTS

Query	Condition
SQL	Join
SQL statement	Multiple joins
SQL clause	De-normalization
Result set	Data warehouse

KEY THEMES

When you have read this chapter, you should be able to define those key concepts in your own words, and you should also be able to:

1. Discuss the structure of an SQL query.
2. Be able to select data from a database using SQL.
3. Be able to join and de-normalize R-tables to create a result set that will form the basis for a management report.

4.1. Introduction

In the two previous chapters we were concerned with the modelling of our management data and with the subsequent storage of these models into R-tables, the underlying foundation of management information systems. We were, however, not particularly concerned with the retrieval of the data once it was stored into the database. To this we shall now turn our attention.

The process of retrieving data from an R-table is called *querying*, and the aim of the current chapter is to explain the basics of querying. Querying of data is done through the provision of instructions to the information system. The instructions are formed using an easy to learn language that specifically deals with the querying of R-tables: it is the so-called *Structured Query Language* (SQL), pronounced 'sequel' by some as Sequel was the original name for SQL. It was first developed in 1974 by Donald Chamberlin and Raymond Boyce, working for IBM. SQL was subsequently standardized by the American National Standards Institute (ANSI) and the International Organization for Standardization (ISO). The latest version is SQL: 2006.

The component of a management information system that handles the processing of SQL queries is called the *SQL parser*. The SQL parser takes in the SQL instructions, and returns the information in the form of a result set. It also warns the user of incomplete or incorrect SQL instructions.

We often speak of *building* queries, because developing a query can be seen as a construction process in which we build up the desired outcome step by step. There are a number of visual query builders available, which use graphical user interfaces to allow you to construct the query. These builders then transform your query into a SQL statement and pass it on to the SQL parser. The benefits of such query builders are somewhat debatable: although you can avoid the use of SQL, and your queries will normally be technically correct, you lose out on flexibility. For any reasonable complex query, it is often recommendable to use the SQL parser directly.

Although SQL is a standardized language, there are a number of variations on the market, with each MIS or database vendor providing a different variant, a so-called *SQL dialect*. Fortunately, the fundamental components of SQL are largely the same in each of these variants, and so we are able to avoid discussion on the specifics of each dialect.

4.2. **Selecting attributes**

SQL consists of a small number of predefined *statements*. The one that we will discuss in this chapter is the SELECT statement. This statement allows us to retrieve data from one or several R-tables.

A SQL statement is composed of different parts called *clauses*. The SELECT statement has a number of clauses and we will discuss each of them in more detail as we proceed through the chapter.

Let us first consider the simple case where we want to retrieve data from one attribute of an R-table, say the R-table `product`. We can display all names from the products that we are selling by issuing a SELECT statement like the following:

```
SELECT name
FROM product
```

You see how straightforward it is to select the attributes: we simply specify the name of the attribute that we want to display in the SELECT clause, and we then add a FROM clause with the name of the R-table from which the attribute originates. The SELECT and the FROM keyword are compulsory for every SELECT statement, and an SQL parser will return an error if they are missing.

The SQL parser returns a list of rows which is known as the *result set*. Let us assume that we will have captured the R-tables from Appendix 1 into our management information system. Issuing the previous query to the SQL parser will then give the following result set:

```
name
======
Orange
Soap
Wine
Apple
Candle
```

The column name in the result set is by default the name of the attribute. If we are unhappy with this, we can change it to another column name using AS, like this:

```
SELECT name AS Product
FROM product
```

This will result in:

```
Product
=======
Orange
Soap
Wine
Apple
Candle
```

An SQL parser will not be able to interpret an SQL command if the R-table names or the attribute names contain blank spaces. Take this command for example:

```
SELECT first name
FROM sales agent
```

This would not work because the SQL parser would think that the space separates the attributes from the FROM keyword. After the second space, the SQL parser would expect the FROM keyword, and it will find name. Because name does not equal to FROM, the parser would provide an error saying this statement is incorrectly specified.

So what if you really insist on having blank spaces in your attribute names, because, for instance, you find that the transaction processing system used them? Most commercially available databases allow you to do so, but they would then require you to encapsulate your attribute names with special characters. This is, for example, possible in one SQL dialect:

```
SELECT [first name]
FROM [sales agent]
```

Or, in another dialect:

```
SELECT 'first name'
FROM 'sales agent'
```

A better way, however, is to use the underscore to represent spaces in attributes and R-table names (as in first_name and sales_agent). This will avoid any use of specific dialects, which is good if you would want to change from one commercial database to another.

For purposes of clarity, each clause is usually listed on a different line. This is however not required. An SQL parser would also accept the entire statement on a single line, for example, SELECT name FROM product. For some SQL parsers, you need to end an SQL statement with a semicolon (;) to let the parser know that you have finished constructing the query.

By convention, the SQL statements are uppercase. This is not strictly required either. Typing select or SeLeCt would also be fine. But by putting the statements in uppercase, it is easier to tell apart the SQL keywords from the attributes and R-tables.

Now moving on to the second case, where we want to select more than one attribute. We would specify that as follows:

```
SELECT name, price
FROM product
```

This would give the following query result:

```
name    price
====== =====
Orange 1
Soap   5
Wine   10
Apple  1
Candle 7
```

Note that the order of the attribute now matters. The query result will have the attributes in the order that you have specified in your SELECT statement.

If we had wanted *all* attributes that are available in a given R-table, we would use an asterisk (*), and the query would look as follows:

```
SELECT *
FROM sales_team
```

This would select all attributes of the entities that are stored in this R-table:

```
team_id name
======= ======
1       Alpha
2       Beta
3       Gamma
```

At this point we should pay close attention to the order in which the instances are ranked in the list. In R-tables, the order of attributes and entities is undefined, and the SQL parser can return the entities in any conceivable order. At the moment, the rows are ordered by the primary key, team_id, but this is an arbitrary choice. We will always need to be explicit about ordering entities if we feel that they should be ordered. We do so using the ORDER BY clause.

For example, if I wanted to have a list of products and prices ordered by price, this is what I would specify:

```
SELECT name, price
FROM product
ORDER BY price
```

This gives the following query result:

```
name    price
======  =====
Orange  1
Apple   1
Soap    5
Candle  7
Wine    10
```

We can sort the entities using more than one attribute in the ORDER BY clause. For example, ORDER BY price, name would sort the entities first by price, and then by name. The default way of ordering is using ascending scale (from lowest to highest). If you want descending scale (from highest to lowest), you can specify this using the extra keyword DESC.

It is possible to not display the attributes on which the entities are to be sorted. So, for example, this is how we would specify a product list without price, but in descending price order, starting from the most expensive to the cheapest price.

```
SELECT name
FROM product
ORDER BY price DESC, name
```

This gives the following query result:

```
name
======
Wine
Candle
Soap
Apple
Orange
```

Note that the instance Apple now comes before the instance Orange because our query specifies that the order should be alphabetical using the product name if the instances have the same price.

4.3. **Selecting specific instances**

The SELECT statement will normally provide us with all the instances that are in the R-table. We are, however, frequently interested in a subset of these instances. We specify the subset by introducing a so-called *condition*. If an instance meets the condition, the instance is included in the subset. If it does not, it is excluded.

Here are four examples of conditions:

```
1. price > 5
2. order_id = 1
3. name = 'Apple'
4. date > '1 Jan 2000'
```

Such conditions are otherwise known as *Boolean expressions*, named after the British mathematician George Boole. A Boolean expression is always TRUE or FALSE.

You need to add the Boolean expression to the SELECT statement using a new clause, WHERE. The WHERE clause always comes after the FROM clause, but before the ORDER BY clause. Here is an example:

```
SELECT name, price
FROM product
WHERE price > 5
ORDER BY price
```

This gives the following query result:

```
name   price
====== =====
Candle 7
Wine   10
```

I need to point out a few special cases in formulating these expressions. The expressions for attributes with type Number are straightforward. You specify simply whether the attribute should be equal to, smaller than, or greater than that particular value (e.g. price > 5). For text, the options are typically limited to equals (=), does not equal (!=), and special cases such as starts with, the format of which unfortunately varies per SQL dialect. Note that you need to specify the value of the text attribute in single or double quotes.

An attribute of type Date or Time is also frequently used in Boolean expressions. Here, the operators 'equal to', 'larger than', and 'smaller than' have the special meaning of 'at the time when', 'after', and 'before', respectively. So, the expression `date > '1 Jan 2000'` indicates all sales that were created *after* 1 Jan 2000.

The True/False attribute type is a special type because it can serve as a Boolean expression without needing to mention anything else. For example, the following query:

```
SELECT name, on_probation
FROM sales_agent
WHERE on_probation
```

This will select all sales agents currently on probation.

We can string together Boolean expressions using AND and OR. AND implies that *all* conditions need to be true for the instance to be included in the subset. OR implies that *any* of the conditions need to be true for the entity to be included in the subset. Whenever we use AND and OR, we need to encapsulate our expressions with brackets '(" and ")'.

This is best explained by an example. Let us assume that I have the following R-table of `line_item`, generated with `SELECT * FROM line_item`.

```
item_id order_id product_id quantity
======= ======== ========== ========
1       1        1          50
2       1        3          50
3       2        1          10
4       3        4          10
5       3        1          75
```

Using the AND clause, I can select those line items involving apples (`product_id = 1`) with a quantity of more than 25.

```
SELECT *
FROM line_item
WHERE (product_id = 1) AND (quantity > 25)
```

This will result in:

```
item_id order_id product_id quantity
======= ======== ========== ========
1       1        1          50
5       3        1          75
```

Had I used the OR keyword, I would have selected all line items involving *either* apples *or* those involving a quantity of more than 25:

```
SELECT *
FROM line_item
WHERE (product_id = 1) OR (quantity > 25)
```

This will result in:

```
item_id order_id product_id quantity
======= ======== ========== ========
1       1        1          50
2       1        3          50
3       2        1          10
5       3        1          75
```

Sometimes it is useful to express a condition in a negative form, that is, we specify the condition and we want to see the entities that do *not* satisfy that particular condition. In that case we would simply put NOT in front of the expression. For example,

```
SELECT *
FROM line_item
WHERE NOT (product_id = 1)
```

This would result in a list of line items that involved anything but apples:

```
item_id order_id product_id quantity
======= ======== ========== ========
2       1        3          50
4       3        4          10
```

4.4. **Joining R-tables**

I will now move on to a somewhat more complicated case, which is a query in which I will incorporate information from another R-table. The conventional name for this type of query is a *joined* query, or simply a *join*. We will first be joining R-tables from entities that have a one-to-many relationship with each other.

For example, let us assume that I want to display the list of sales agents and the names of the teams to which they belong. Let me first list the R-tables separately. SELECT agent_id, name, team_id FROM sales_agent ORDER BY agent_id results in:

```
agent_id name   team_id
======== ====   =======
1        Jim    1
2        Tom    2
3        Mary   1
4        Jim    2
5        Jack   NULL
```

And SELECT team_id, name FROM sales_team ORDER BY team_id results in:

```
team_id name
======= =====
1       Alpha
2       Beta
3       Gamma
```

I would now like to combine these two tables, so that I can start combining the names of the sales teams with the names of the sales agents. We would have to start with something like this.

```
SELECT name, name
FROM sales_agent, sales_team
```

This will obviously confuse the SQL parser, as it would not be able to tell which name attribute belongs to which table. Whenever there is such confusion, the SQL parser will return an error saying that the attribute names are ambiguous. The solution is to prefix the attribute with the name of the respective R-table, like this:

```
SELECT sales_agent.name, sales_team.name
FROM sales_agent, sales_team
```

This will result in:

```
sales_agent.name sales_team.name
================ ===============
Jim              Alpha
Jim              Beta
Jim              Gamma
Tom              Alpha
Tom              Beta
Tom              Gamma
Mary             Alpha
Mary             Beta
Mary             Gamma
Jim              Alpha
Jim              Beta
Jim              Gamma
Jack             Alpha
Jack             Beta
Jack             Gamma
```

What the SQL parser tries to do is list all the possible *combinations* of the two entities. It is associating every entity in one R-table with an entity in the other R-table. So, every sales agent is connected to every team. Because we had 5 entities in our sales_agent table, and 3 entities in our sales_team table, the query returns 5 times 3 = 15 possible combinations. We would thus say the SQL parser provides the *product* of the two tables.

I will extend the above query slightly so that you can see how the one-to-many query is beginning to be shaped.

```
SELECT sales_agent.name, sales_agent.team_id,
sales_team.team_id, sales_team.name
FROM sales_agent, sales_team
```

This will result in:

```
agent.name agent.team_id team.team_id team.name
========== ============= ============ =========
Jim        1             1            Alpha
Jim        1             2            Beta
```

```
Jim      1        3        Gamma
Tom      2        1        Alpha
Tom      2        2        Beta
Tom      2        3        Gamma
Mary     1        1        Alpha
Mary     1        2        Beta
Mary     1        3        Gamma
Jim      2        1        Alpha
Jim      2        2        Beta
Jim      2        3        Gamma
Jack     NULL     1        Alpha
Jack     NULL     2        Beta
Jack     NULL     3        Gamma
```

You can see that nothing special really happened. We simply added more attributes from the R-tables that we have multiplied. So there are still 15 rows of data, each connecting one entity (an agent) to another (a team). But you can also see that the foreign key and the primary key sometimes match. This happens in 4 of the 15 rows. We can use this information to create the following SELECT command:

```
SELECT sales_agent.name, sales_team.name
FROM sales_agent, sales_team
WHERE sales_agent.team_id = sales_team.team_id
```

This will result in the following subset:

```
agent.name team.name
========== =========
Jim        Alpha
Tom        Beta
Mary       Alpha
Jim        Beta
```

We can change both the order of the attributes and the order of the entities to provide a nicer report:

```
SELECT sales_team.name, sales_agent.name
FROM sales_agent, sales_team
WHERE sales_agent.team_id = sales_team.team_id
ORDER BY sales_team.name, sales_agent.name
```

This will result in the following result set:

```
team.name agent.name
========= ==========
Alpha     Jim
Alpha     Mary
Beta      Jim
Beta      Tom
```

Let me briefly summarize what I have done. I have used the primary key and the foreign key from a one-to-many relationship to join the attribute information of two R-tables. First, you select the product of the two R-tables. You then use a WHERE clause to equate the foreign key of the first R-table with the primary key of the second R-table. You then order the attributes and entities as you see fit.

This is a commonly used method, but it is not without problems. For example, what happened to Jack? He did not belong to a team and so he disappeared. What happened to the Gamma team? It did not have any agents in the data set and so it disappeared. You see that this method does not really work in case the one-to-many relationship is optional. In that case it is possible that an instance (such as Jack) will have a foreign key of value NULL. Consequently, the expression that compares the foreign key to an existing primary key will always be FALSE.

To resolve these problems, there is a special JOIN clause available in the SQL language. This JOIN clause can be used to make sure that data from optional relationships is also included. There are different types of JOINs such as INNER JOIN, LEFT JOIN, and RIGHT JOIN. The detailed treatment of the JOIN clause is outside the scope of this book, and I will have to refer to more dedicated SQL books for more detail on them.

4.5. **Multiple joins and de-normalization**

So far I have been discussing two tables only, to deal with one one-to-many relationship. I will now move on to the case where I have more than one foreign key in an R-table. This will involve the joining of multiple tables.

You will encounter this case with an entity that was previously identified in the context of a many-to-many relationship. For example, the line item entity was used to remove a many-to-many relationship between sales orders and products. The line item connects sales orders and products, and so any query that displays some information about the line items will need to display data from the sales order and from the product.

You will also encounter this case in situations where you have strings of primary and foreign keys, such as the one I have been discussing in Chapter 2 on page 32. For example, if you are joining the sales orders and the sales agents, displaying the sales agent's name with every sales order, you will see that it is possible to display the foreign key of the sales team as well. So, another join is needed with the sales team table to make sure that you do not display an identity attribute, but the name of the sales team.

When we start joining the attributes of multiple tables in this way, we will eventually end up with a result set that has all non-identity attributes involved in the initial R-table. This process is called *data de-normalization*. During de-normalization, all the foreign keys are removed step by step. The following list demonstrates how de-normalization works and what it looks like when the line item table is de-normalized.

Start with initial R-table: We start with the R-table `line_item`. There are obviously foreign keys to the sales order and to the product.

First-order joins: Let us first remove the foreign key `order_id` by joining the sales order attributes. There is now significant data redundancy in the data set. Also, the table contains two new foreign keys, for customer and for sales agent.

We need to remove a second foreign key that we started out with, the `product_id`. By joining the `product` R-table, we receive in return the attributes for the products, such as product name and product price. We also receive a new foreign key, one that refers to the product type.

Second-order joins: These joins involve the removal of the foreign keys that entered the result set when we joined the neighbouring R-tables. In our example, they involve the joining of the tables `customer`, `sales_agent`, and `product_type`. Are we done? Not quite, because by joining these tables we have introduced once again new foreign keys. They are `team_id` and `status_id`.

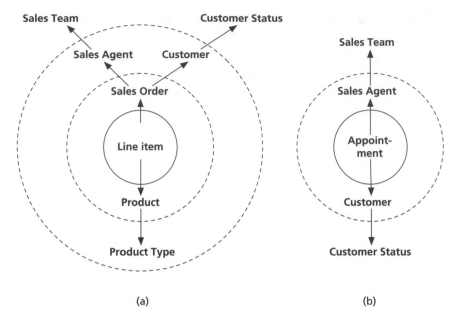

Figure 1 De-normalization

Third-order joins: Now we also join the sales team and the customer status with the original line item table. We are done. There are no more foreign keys in our result set.

De-normalization, that is, ironing out all foreign keys, is a process that can be visualized using concentric circles, as in Figure 1a, where I have de-normalized the line item table.

De-normalization will give us a so-called *de-normalized* result set with all non-identity attributes associated with the initial R-table. An example of what such a result set could look like, given the data from Appendix 1, is displayed in Table 4.1.

In this example I have not included *all* attributes that we would be able to access, but only some of them that could be relevant for us later on. Note that the appointment R-table does not feature in this final result set. That is because there is no appointment data connected to the line item data using a foreign key. Had we wanted to de-normalize the appointment table, we would do so using the process visualized in Figure 1b. I leave this as an exercise for you.

Table 4.1 Source data for a management information system

Item	Order	Customer	Product	Category	Price	Quantity	Agent	Sales Team	Date
1	1	Cyndi	Orange	Food	1	6	Jim	Alpha	3 Jan
2	1	Cyndi	Candle	Non-Food	7	34	Jim	Alpha	3 Jan
3	2	Kasey	Wine	Food	10	24	Mary	Alpha	7 Jan
4	2	Kasey	Orange	Food	1	4	Mary	Alpha	7 Jan
5	2	Kasey	Apple	Food	1	35	Mary	Alpha	7 Jan
6	3	Evelyne	Orange	Food	1	13	Tom	Beta	8 Jan
7	3	Evelyne	Soap	Non-Food	5	19	Tom	Beta	8 Jan
8	4	Ocean	Apple	Food	1	30	Jim	Alpha	9 Jan
9	4	Ocean	Soap	Non-Food	5	9	Jim	Alpha	9 Jan
10	5	Joan	Soap	Non-Food	5	14	Jim	Beta	11 Jan
11	5	Joan	Wine	Food	10	16	Jim	Beta	11 Jan
12	6	Myra	Apple	Food	1	21	Mary	Alpha	15 Jan
13	6	Myra	Orange	Food	1	8	Mary	Alpha	15 Jan
14	7	Godfrey	Candle	Non-Food	7	33	Tom	Beta	17 Jan
15	8	Celeste	Wine	Food	10	20	Mary	Alpha	21 Jan
16	8	Celeste	Candle	Non-Food	7	32	Mary	Alpha	21 Jan
17	9	Lennard	Apple	Food	1	26	Jim	Beta	29 Jan
18	10	Justin	Soap	Non-Food	5	15	Tom	Beta	30 Jan
19	10	Justin	Wine	Food	10	17	Tom	Beta	30 Jan
20	10	Justin	Candle	Non-Food	7	7	Tom	Beta	30 Jan

To generate these tables, the SQL parser has had to generate a product of the original tables. In the previous example, there are 20 line items, 10 sales orders, 10 customers, 5 products, 2 product categories, 4 sales agents, and 2 sales teams. This implies that the resulting product is $20 \times 10 \times 10 \times 5 \times 2 \times 4 \times 2 = 160,000$ possible combinations. That is very many considering that we only had very few instances to start out with. You will appreciate that in a real-life management scenario, the number of combinations ends up in millions. Computing performance of the SQL parser is therefore often a big problem in management information systems.

The problem of SQL JOIN performance often takes the form of *query plan optimization*. It is possible for the SQL Parser, by looking at the SQL query carefully, to find ways to speed up query processing. For example, by analysing which foreign keys need to be matched, it would not have to produce a full product of all the R-tables, but would rather generate a subset of that full product in which the foreign keys are matched already. Commercial vendors of database software often compete with each other on query plan performance.

The *data warehouse* concept that we have discussed in Chapter 1 can now be further specified. A data warehouse is a select set of de-normalized R-tables, taken from the R-tables in the transaction processing systems. These data warehouse tables can be seen as the result of pre-processing data, to be used by a management information system. The pre-processing is necessary because of the severe performance problems that we often encounter. The tables can be used by management information systems, and we will often find that they refer to these tables as the 'raw data' for any managerial report.

☐ FURTHER READING

In this chapter I have demonstrated the use of SQL, an easy to use language to query data from a transaction processing system. SQL produces result sets: lists of rows that are taken from the R-tables. These result sets eventually form the basis for our management reports.

There is more to SQL than the SELECT statement. Explaining the full range of SQL statements is outside the scope of this book, but more information can be found in Van der Lans (1989), and of course on the Internet where many other tutorials are available.

5 Aggregating data

KEY THEMES

When you have read this chapter, you should be able to define those key concepts in your own words, and you should also be able to:

1. Understand the basic manipulations on a de-normalized result set.
2. Outline and discuss the different ways to aggregate data.
3. Connect the different options to aggregate data with the different types of measurement scales.
4. Construct summary tables, cross-tabulations, and pivot tables using the result set manipulations and the aggregation options.

5.1. Introduction

In the previous chapter we have seen how you can query databases to get result sets of individual instances. We shall now concern ourselves with generating data about *groups* of instances. We shall refer to this as *aggregated data*. Examples of such information include the total revenue on our sales orders, the average volume of sales, the maximum quantity in a particular month, and so on.

It goes without saying that aggregating data effectively is an essential skill for a manager. A management information system should be able to support aggregation rapidly and accurately, and ideally in a somewhat flexible way, as there are many different ways to aggregate data.

How do we generate aggregated data? First of all, SQL can be of assistance. It is possible to use the SQL language to select information about groups of entities. For example, SQL features a GROUP BY clause, as well as aggregated functions such as SUM, AVG, MAX, and so on. Normally, however, we would leave the SQL parser behind at this point, and focus on the spreadsheet environment, or use a dedicated business intelligence or data warehouse package.

The reasons why we are turning to spreadsheets and dedicated business intelligence software at this stage are twofold. First, these tools have more advanced aggregation functions. For example, they have interactive functionalities such as pivot tables, to be discussed in this chapter. Second, these tools are equipped with more powerful visualization techniques. I shall talk more about visualization in the next chapter. While databases are splendid tools to capture and organize transaction data, we would move to spreadsheets and business intelligence tools to deal with aggregated data.

In this chapter I shall first review the fundamentals of data aggregation, and then move on to the basic structures to aggregate. These include the construction of the summary table, the cross-tab, and finally the pivot table.

5.2. **Manipulating aggregated tables**

Let us return to where we ended in the last chapter, which was with the creation of a de-normalized table that contained a set of transaction data. Such tables represent collections of attributes from different R-tables, joined together in large tables, ready for further analysis.

These intermediate tables are so vital to the generation of adequate management information that they have some specific terminology associated with them. I need to introduce you to this terminology first before I can move on with the rest of the material.

First, it is common to refer to the columns of these tables as *variables*. A variable has a range of values, and each variable represents one *dimension*. This is the reason why these tables are also called *multidimensional tables*. The dimensions in question refer to the columns of the table. The fact that these columns were originally represented as attributes in different R-tables need no longer concern us here.

The de-normalized tables are typically very large, and they contain a large number of columns and a large number of rows. In order to make sense of the data, we would typically reduce the table to something that is more meaningful to grasp. This is called table manipulation, and the ways that we manipulate these tables also have some terminology associated with them.

The first manipulation on these tables is to select only a subset of rows. This would be a similar exercise to the one in the previous chapter where we used the WHERE clause in the SQL statement. The term used for selecting a subset of rows in a multidimensional table is called *slicing*. We 'slice' the table by removing a number of rows that, for one reason or another, do not interest us. In our sales management example, we could, for example, just select the transaction data that pertains to sales team Alpha.

The second manipulation on these tables is to select only a subset of columns (dimensions). This is called *dicing*. We 'dice' the table by removing the columns that, for one reason or another, do not interest us. For example, we might not be interested in the names of the sales agents, and in that case we would remove those columns.

Together, these two operations on the table allows us to 'slice and dice' the multidimensional table to a table that is smaller and that would better serve our purposes. Figure 1 displays graphically the two operations at work. The slicing operation shows how we remove the rows that do not

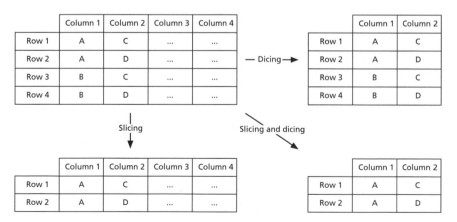

Figure 1 Slicing and dicing

have value A in the first column. The dicing operation shows how we remove the columns that do not interest us.

The third and fourth type of manipulation on these tables deal with the aggregation itself. We can 'collapse' a number of rows by replacing them with one row, and have appropriate aggregate values to 'represent' the underlying individual values. For example, let us suppose we have sliced and diced Table 4.1 into the following table:

Table 5.1 Sample table with transaction data

Order	Customer	Product	Price	Quantity
1	Cyndi	Orange	1	6
1	Cyndi	Candle	7	34
2	Kasey	Wine	10	24
2	Kasey	Orange	1	4
2	Kasey	Apple	1	35

I could then 'collapse' these five rows into two rows by grouping them according to order (order 1 and order 2). This would result in

Table 5.2 Sample table rolled up by order

Order	Customer	Product	Average price	Total quantity
1	Cyndi	–	4	40
2	Kasey	–	4	63

Alternatively, I could collapse these five rows into four rows by grouping them according to product. This would result in

Table 5.3 Sample table rolled up by product

Order	Customer	Product	Price	Total quantity
–	–	Orange	1	10
–	–	Candle	7	34
–	–	Wine	10	24
–	–	Apple	1	35

This process of collapsing data into aggregate values is known as *rolling up* data. The opposite of rolling up is *drilling down*. Here, you 'expand' an aggregated value into its underlying transactional values.

In studying these examples please pay attention to the following two aspects. First, you will see that there is no need to supply aggregate values for those variables (attributes) that belong to the original variable that you are grouping the data by. These variables often were originally attributes of the same entity.

Second, you will see that there are different ways to calculate aggregate values: I have used the average and the total here, and you will note that I have not aggregated the product names because averaging and totaling product names would not really make sense. This is not to say there are no other ways of aggregating product names. This is indeed possible, and I will discuss them later in this chapter. It depends on the type of data which aggregate operation you can use.

In sum, the four basic manipulations on a de-normalized table are slicing and dicing, rolling up, and drilling down. Business intelligence packages allow you to perform all these operations in any conceivable order. For example, one could first roll up the line item data by order, then select (dice) the customers, then drill down by customer, and then select (slice) only the most profitable ones.

5.3. **Data aggregation scales**

Before we can start covering the different data aggregation operations, we must first return to the allowable values for our data again. You may remember that we discussed different attribute types in Chapter 2 on page 25. I emphasized there that it is important to specify the range of allowable values for each attribute.

In a similar vein, variables have allowable values. The allowable values of a variable are reflected in the choice of *measurement scale*. The choice of measurement scale is a bit different from the attribute types that we discussed earlier. Because the aggregation operations available to us depend on the measurement scale, it is useful to categorize our data sets adequately so that it is straightforward to see which operation can be used for which type of measurement scale.

A list of the available measurement scales follows. It is a set of scale types first outlined by Stevens (1946).

Nominal scale: Data is measured on a nominal scale if the data can be counted but not ranked. For example, in Table 4.1 on page 61, the product, the product category, the sales agent, and the sales team area are all measured on nominal scales.

In terms of mapping this scale to attribute types, any attribute type of type Text corresponds to the nominal scale, except when the values can be ranked. Attributes from entities that were originally of type Category often fall into this scale.

Ordinal scale: Data is measured on an ordinal scale if the data can be counted and the values can be ranked in a meaningful order. When an attribute has adopted an ordinal scale, it means that we know that the values can be ranked, but the difference between the values is unknown.

Examples include the possible responses to a multiple-choice question such as 'Strongly Disagree', 'Slightly Disagree', 'Neutral', 'Slightly agree', or 'Strongly Agree'. There is a rank order here in the extent to which the respondent agrees with the question. We could say that, on the 'agreeableness' dimension, 'Strongly Agree' is higher ranked then 'Slightly Agree'. Colloquially, we could say that Strongly Agree is 'greater than', or 'better than' Slightly Agree.

With ordinal scales, we know that one value is higher than another, but we do not know how much higher. The difference between the values is unknown and cannot be measured. For example, we would not be able to say precisely how much Strongly Agree is better than Slightly Agree. And we would not be able to measure whether the difference between Strongly Agree and Slightly Agree is greater or smaller than the difference between Slightly Agree and Neutral.

Very often, an ordinal scale can be used for those categorical entities for which we can provide an entity lifecycle, as discussed in Chapter 3. We could rank customer status into Contact, Lead, Promising Lead, Prospect, and Customer. The rank order here is the progress a customer has made in the lifecycle. Cast in this way, we could say that a Prospect is 'greater than' or 'better than' than a Promising Lead.

Interval scale: This is a measurement scale where data can be counted, the values can be ranked, and it is clear how much one data value differs from another.

The most common examples in an MIS setting are the attributes of type Time Stamp. For example, we know that in any specific week, a day on Thursday is 'higher' than a day on Tuesday, and that the difference is exactly two days. A four-month period is exactly twice as long as a two-month period.

The defining characteristic of interval scales is that we can count the values, we can rank them, and we can add and subtract them.

Ratio scale: This is a measurement scale that resembles the interval scale in all aspects, and in addition a value of 0 can be distinctly identified. Such a zero point would denote that no quantity of the attribute was present.

In an MIS setting, examples of measurement on ratio scales are sales volume and price. A sales volume of 0 would mean that no products were sold, a clear zero point. Price is another example. A price of 0 would mean that no money was being asked for the product. That, too, is a clear zero point. Indeed all attributes of type Number would normally qualify.

The presence of a zero point is important because this is the one thing that distinguishes the ratio scale from the interval scale. It enables us to multiply and divide data values, something we could not do with interval scales. Ratio values allow you to express one value as a fraction (a ratio) of another value on that same dimension.

Please note that time stamps are interval-scaled and not ratio-scaled because they do not have a zero point. We obviously have the year 0 but that does not mean that there was no time then. Consequently we cannot divide Wednesday by Tuesday, for example, or express Saturday as a fraction of Sunday.

In summary, the defining characteristic of ratio scales is that we can count the values, we can rank them, we can add and subtract them, and we can divide and multiply them.

An elegant and useful aspect of this classification is that every category also carries the characteristics of its previous category. Every ratio-scaled variable is also an interval-scaled variable. Each interval-scaled variable is also an ordinal-scaled variable. And each ordinal-scaled variable is also a nominal-scaled variable.

At this point I want to clarify some potential areas of confusion that often arise when people are exposed to these different measurement scales for the first time.

First of all, some get a bit confused with the nominal scale because they believe that, for example, sales agents can be ordered alphabetically and so must be ordinal. After all, if you ask the SQL parser to order sales agents by name, that is what it would do, and so it must be ordinal because it can be sorted. You need to keep in mind, however, that such a ranking is really nothing but an arbitrary ordering of the sales agents *by name*. We are not actually ranking sales agents on their 'sales agent-ness'.

Second, students often think that nominal values can be sorted too by taking into account other measures. For example, we can order sales agents on their sales performance, and so sales agents must be ordinal and not nominal? Not really is the answer, because in that case we are actually ranking the sales performance, and implicitly we are combining two attributes, sales agent, and sales performance.

Third, there is often confusion between interval-scales and ratio-scales in that differences between the interval values can be multiplied and divided. For example, twice a two-month period (a difference of two months) is a four-month period (a difference of four months). Thus, the differences can be expressed in ratio-scaled terms.

Finally, there is a subtle difference here between the way we rank data on the ordinal scale and the way we would order data when we retrieve it as a query from an R-table. For example, if we have the following SQL query:

```
SELECT name
FROM customer_status
ORDER BY name
```

The order of the responses would be alphabetical and would, in this case, result in:

```
name
===============
Contact
Customer
Lead
Promising lead
Prospect
```

This ordered result set is hardly what we had in mind for our ordinal scale. The SQL parser does not know how to rank these entities on 'life-cycle stage'. The solution is to create an additional attribute called 'rank', which allows us to sort the instances in the way that we would like. For example, this query

```
SELECT rank, name
FROM customer_status
ORDER BY rank
```

would result in:

```
rank name
==== ===============
1    Contact
2    Lead
3    Promising Lead
4    Prospect
5    Customer
```

5.4. **Aggregation options**

Having equipped ourselves with the correct terminology, we are now able to concern ourselves with the construction of aggregated values.

An aggregated value is a value that represents a group of values of the same attribute but from different entities. For example, if we had the individual values 2, 4, and 6 (denoting, say, the price of three products), then the aggregated value could be 12. In this case, that value would represent the sum of the values. Another aggregated value could be 4, which would represent the mean of the three values.

What follows is a list of options to aggregate data for a variable. As we discussed previously, the measurement scale of a variable is an important determinant in the aggregation options that we have at our disposal.

Count: Also known as frequency. This category refers to the number that specific data values occur in the data set. For example, we could count the number of times that specific sales agents appear in Table 4.1.

Frequency can be used with all types of variables. It is one of the few aggregate options available to nominal-scaled variables.

Minimum, Maximum: Provides the lowest or highest value in the rank. As you can see, the variable needs to be scaled on a rank for this to be meaningful, and thus nominal-scaled variables drop out here. This option is only available for ordinal-scaled variables and up.

Total: This is the overall value when all data values are summed up. Of course this only has meaning when the data values are actually amenable to numerical calculation, including at least the option to add and subtract the values. Thus, the totaling option is only available for interval- and ratio-scaled variables.

Average: Also known as central tendency. The measures of central tendency provide aggregate information about the *centre* of the distribution of the values.

We have different measures of average depending on the measurement scale. For a nominal-scaled variable, the appropriate aggregate measure in this category is the *mode*. The mode is the value that occurs the most. For ordinal-scaled variables, it is the *median*. The median is the value that represents the exact middle. For interval- and ratio-scaled variables, this value is the *mean* (abbreviated M). The mean represents the arithmetic average of the values present.

Variation: The measures of variation provide information about the *spread* of data around the centre. This does not apply to nominal-scaled variables, because there is no centre. For ordinal-scaled variables, we can identify the so-called *interquartile range*, or IQR. This is the range of values that represent the middle half of the values available. For interval- and ratio-scaled variables, the archetypical measure of variation is the *standard deviation* (abbreviated SD). The standard deviation measures how close or how far data is to the mean.

Shape: The aggregate measures of shape describe in more detail the way in which the data is spread around the centre. Kurtosis and skewness are the best known measures here for interval- and ratio-scaled variables. Kurtosis refers to 'peakedness' or 'flatness' of the data distribution: the higher the kurtosis, the closer data is to the mean and the less data is further away from the mean. Skewness refers to the symmetry of the shape. Skewness measures identify whether there is more data on one side of the mean than on the other. The aggregate measures of shape are little used in comparison to the other aggregate measures.

5.5. **Summary tables and frequency tables**

An important concept in data aggregation is the *derived attribute*. The derived attribute is an attribute the values of which combine or manipulate other values from the same instance in a predefined way. For example, we could create an attribute called 'Revenue', the values of which we could define as the value of the attribute 'Price' times the value of the attribute 'Quantity'. The derived value is, if you like, a 'ghost' value: it is never actually stored in a data set, but because we know the definition of how it is calculated, we would always be able to generate it should we want to.

Note that a derived value always refers to one instance, and is not to be mistaken for an aggregation value. Remember that an aggregation value always combines the values of more than one instance. Table 5.4 illustrates the difference. You see in this table the line items for sales order 1. The derived attribute Revenue is displayed as the last column, in italics to indicate its 'ghost' status. The derived values are 6 (6 oranges sold at

Table 5.4 Derived and aggregated values

Order	Product	Price	Quantity	Revenue
1	Orange	1	6	*6*
1	Candle	7	34	*238*
				244

price 1) and 238 (34 candles sold at price 7). The aggregation value is 244 (using the option total), representing the combined values of 6 and 238.

We can also manipulate time stamp attributes in this way. We can, for example, create a derived attribute called 'Week.' Table 5.5 provides the week number for each sales order. It is through the use of derived attributes that we can implement changes in the format of the attribute, as discussed previously in Chapter 2 on page 26.

Spreadsheets are powerful tools to create derived values using definitions called *formulas*. Formulas can make reference to cells (intersections of rows and columns), and can be copied and pasted in flexible ways.

We can now proceed with constructing *summary tables*. A summary table provides aggregate data of one attribute grouped by the values of another attribute. The summary table provides a subset of the columns (usually just the attribute value with the nominal scale) as well as the rows. In that sense, it is a condensed view of the de-normalized result set that we developed in the previous chapter.

Let me give a few illustrations of summary tables that take Table 4.1 as its origin. We can, for example, look at the sales revenue by sales order. Table 5.6 illustrates what such a summary looks like. I have selected for my subset the columns Sales Order, Sales Agent, Sales Team, and Revenue. Note that the derived values for revenue provide the subtotal of the line items that contributed to this order.

I could summarize this table even further by grouping the line item data not just by order, but also by sales agent. Table 5.7 illustrates this. And it is

Table 5.5 Derived attribute week number

Order	Date	Week
1	3 Jan	1
2	7 Jan	2
3	8 Jan	2
4	9 Jan	2
5	11 Jan	2
6	15 Jan	3
7	17 Jan	3
8	21 Jan	4
9	29 Jan	5
10	30 Jan	5

Table 5.6 Sum of sales revenue broken down by sales order

Order	Agent	Team	*Revenue*
1	Jim	Alpha	*244*
2	Mary	Alpha	*279*
3	Tom	Beta	*108*
4	Jim	Alpha	*75*
5	Jim	Beta	*230*
6	Mary	Alpha	*29*
7	Tom	Beta	*231*
8	Mary	Alpha	*424*
9	Jim	Beta	*26*
10	Tom	Beta	*294*
			1,940

straightforward to summarize this even further, and group by sales team, as Table 5.8 illustrates.

You will perhaps have recognized that the breakdown pattern follows the string of one-to-many relationships that you can identify in the ER diagram in Figure 10 of Chapter 2 on page 34. We grouped the revenue for an individual line item into an order, we grouped that by agent, and we grouped that by team. You should always be able to group your data in this way.

Business intelligence systems allow you to summarize and 'de-summarize' the data interactively. You can, for example, go from Table 5.7 to Table 5.8 (rolling up, or aggregating the data). You can also go back from Table 5.8 to Table 5.7 (de-aggregating, or drilling down).

Table 5.7 Sum of sales revenue broken down by sales agent

Agent	Team	*Revenue*
Jim	Alpha	*319*
Mary	Alpha	*732*
Tom	Beta	*633*
Jim	Beta	*256*
		1,940

Table 5.8 Sum of sales revenue broken down by sales team

Team	Revenue
Alpha	1,051
Beta	889
	1,940

So far we have looked at summary tables that used nominal-scaled variables to drill-down and roll-up the data. We can of course also use other variables. Let us first examine an interval-scaled variable, such as time stamp. The week number can provide us a vehicle to split and aggregate the data, as Table 5.9 shows.

A special version of a summary table is the *frequency table*. In a frequency table, the values of an attribute are grouped in one column, and the second column indicates the number of occurrences of each of those values in the original result set. Table 5.10 provides an example for a variable on a nominal scale, the product.

We could also construct frequency tables for interval and ratio-scale variables. In that case we would identify so-called *bins*. Bins are chopped up parts of the scale, carefully constructed so that they represent the entire range along which variables are measured. Each bin represents an equal portion of the scale. When the bins are constructed, you can subsequently count the number of data values that fall within each bin.

Take for example the derived attribute Revenue. If you calculate revenue for every line item, you would have 20 derived values, ranging from

Table 5.9 Sum of sales revenue broken down by week number

Week	Revenue
1	244
2	692
3	260
4	424
5	320
	1,940

Table 5.10 Count of products sold by product sold

Product	Count
Orange	4
Apple	4
Wine	4
Soap	4
Candle	4
	20

4 (line item 4) to 240 (line item 3). We could identify 5 bins, each bin representing 50. Table 5.11 presents the corresponding frequency table.

5.6. **Cross-tabulations and pivot tables**

A *cross-tabulation*, or more colloquially, *cross-tab*, is a summary table for two dimensions. You would have the same aggregated value, but it is mapped out in rows and mapped out in columns. Table 5.12 for example, provides us an overview of sales revenue per team and per month. Before you proceed please study carefully how this cross-tab is a combination of two summary tables, Tables 5.7 and 5.9, respectively.

In another example, we can examine the count of products and the count of the revenue bins and map them together in a cross-tabulation like the one in Table 5.13. Again, before moving on, please study carefully how this cross-tab is a combination of Tables 5.10 and 5.11.

Table 5.11 Count of revenue by revenue bin

Revenue	Count
0–50	10
51–100	3
101–150	0
151–200	3
201–250	4
	20

Table 5.12 Cross-tabulation of sales revenue broken down by sales agent and by week

Agent	Team	Week 1	Week 2	Week 3	Week 4	Week 5	Total
Jim	Alpha	244	75	0	0	0	319
Mary	Alpha	0	279	29	424	0	732
Tom	Beta	0	108	231	0	294	633
Jim	Beta	0	230	0	0	26	256
		244	692	260	424	320	1,940

The value of the cross-tabulation is that it provides insight into the relationship between the two variables in which the cross-tab breaks down the total number. For example, Table 5.12 gives us some insight in the activities of the sales agents over the weeks. We can see that Jim from Team Alpha was really successful in Weeks 1 and 2 and then did not secure any sales orders. Such information was not readily visible from the data set in Table 4.1. Likewise, we can study Table 5.13 and identify that the bigger sales orders are wines and candles only. We could have suspected that relationship given their more expensive prices, but it is confirmed by the data, and that was not immediately identifiable in Table 4.1.

Please be aware that the rows and columns of the cross-tab have decidedly different meanings than the rows and columns from an R-table or an SQL result set. In an R-table, the columns referred to attributes of entities and the rows referred to instances of those entities. In a cross-tab, *both*

Table 5.13 Cross-tabulation of products sold broken down by revenue and by product sold

Revenue	Orange	Apple	Wine	Soap	Candle	Count
0–50	4	4	0	1	1	10
51–100	0	0	0	3	0	3
101–150	0	0	0	0	0	0
151–200	0	0	3	0	0	3
201–250	0	0	1	0	3	4
	4	4	4	4	4	20

Table 5.14 Cross-tabulation of products sold broken down by revenue and by product sold

Revenue	0–50	51–100	101–150	151–200	201–250	Count
Orange	4	0	0	0	0	4
Apple	4	0	0	0	0	4
Wine	0	0	0	3	1	4
Soap	1	3	0	0	0	4
Candle	1	0	0	0	3	4
	10	3	0	3	4	20

the rows and the columns now refer to aggregate attribute values. There is nothing that would prevent us from turning the cross-tab around, that is, specify the attribute week as the row and the attributes teams and agents as columns. Table 5.14 demonstrates what this looks like.

The choice of rows and columns is not a completely arbitrary affair though. There is an important relationship between the choice of rows and columns in data aggregation, and the choice of X-axis and Y-axis in data visualization. I will discuss this some more in the next chapter on data visualization.

A *pivot table* is the interactive cousin of the cross-tabulation. It is one of the most powerful tools available in spreadsheets. The pivot table allows us to create cross-tabs interactively. We spoke earlier about 'turning' the data, that is, swapping rows and columns as we saw fit. It is the idea of turning the data around a pivot from where the pivot table draws its name.

To create a pivot table, we would normally start out with a table like the one in Table 4.1. The spreadsheet would then allow us to provide the variable that we want to aggregate (in our case, the derived variable Revenue). It would then give us the aggregation options, from Section 5.4 such as Count and Sum.

Given the aggregated variable and the aggregation option, a pivot table can be dynamically created by choosing different variables as rows and as columns. For example, it would be easy to switch from Table 5.13 to Table 5.14. We would simply drag and drop the Revenue bin from the column to the row, and vice-versa.

⬚ FURTHER READING

Standard textbooks on business statistics and business research methods provide ample description of aggregated functions (see e.g. Saunders, Lewis, and Thornhill 2006; Berenson, Levine, and Krehbiel 2005).

An interesting study on the effects of data aggregation is the one by Chervany et al. (1974). In this experiment two groups of students played a management simulated game at the University of Minnesota. The first group had access to all the unaggregated data that came from the fictional company. The second group only had access to the aggregated data: means, standard deviations, minimum, and maximum. Eventually, the second group performed better in terms of objective company performance, that is, revenue and profit. However, the *subjective* decision performance decreased: the participants were *less* confident about whether they had made the right decisions.

It is thus important to provide extensive drill-down options, so that managers can always go back to the unaggregated data should they wish to do so.

6 Visualizing data

KEY THEMES

When you have read this chapter, you should be able to define those key concepts in your own words, and you should also be able to:

1. Choose the right chart for the right type of variable or set of variables.
2. Understand the danger of suggesting dependency when in fact there is none.
3. Discuss the advantages and disadvantages of adding colour.
4. Resist the urge to dress up your charts with pretty effects.

6.1. Introduction

In the previous chapter, we have been concerned with the construction of aggregate tables: frequency tables, summary tables, cross-tabulations, and pivot tables. We shall now move on to the visualization of these tables. Although charts often use aggregated data as the basis, it is also possible to visualize transaction data without any aggregation.

The visualization of data has been described as the 'front line of attack' to explore patterns in data (Cleveland 1993). It helps us understand trends that are not easily spotted in aggregated tables. Also, it helps to compress large amounts of data, and, in doing so, helps to avoid information overload.

The value of charts over tables has been demonstrated in an experiment where students played a simulation game to manage inventory levels (Benbasat and Schroeder 1977). Half of the students had to base their decisions on output in table format. The other half had to base their decisions on charts. The students with the charts significantly outperformed the students with the tables.

There is an interesting asymmetry between data presented in tabular format and data presented in graphical format. Although one can always transform the tabular format into the graphical format, the reverse is not always true without losing some precision. This, then, is the trade-off when you balance the graphical or tabular formats: you win on understanding, but you lose on precision. When both are important, most users tend to prefer receiving both formats rather than one or the other (Benbasat and Dexter 1986).

Charts can be categorized according to the number of attributes that are represented at the same time. In this chapter I will first discuss the charts that visualize the values of one variable. I will then move on to two variables, particularly summary tables and cross tabs. After that I will discuss the visualization of three or more variables and take you through several techniques to do so. I will end with discussing dynamic charts, and the use of colour and other visual effects.

6.2. **Visualizing one variable**

The simplest charts are the *univariate charts*, those that visualize a set of values of one particular variable. Let us first consider the case where the variable is measured on an ordinal, interval, or ratio-scale. These measurement scales are sufficiently informative for us to plot the data values on an axis. Both the individual data and the aggregation data can be used to plot the variable on an axis. We would say that the axis represents one *dimension*, and that the chart is therefore unidimensional.

Figure 1 shows examples of three common charts for plotting ordinal, interval, and ratio variables on an axis. To generate these univariate charts I have used the data from the variable Quantity from Table 4.1.

Figure 1a represents a *dot scale*, which plots each value as a dot on the scale of the variable. This gives us an insight in the distribution of the individual data values on the entire range of values.

The dot scale starts to loose its value when you have a large number of data points and the distribution of values along the axis becomes blurry. In

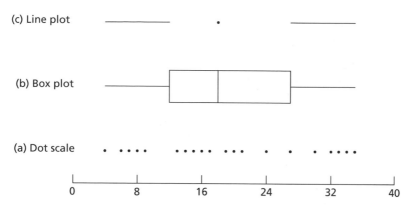

Figure 1 Dot scale, box plot, and line plot

that case you can resort to plotting the statistical aggregation measures. As discussed in the previous chapter, for ordinal, interval, and ratio variables we can use the minimum, the maximum, the first quartile, the median, and the third quartile. The *box plot*, invented by John Tukey (1977), plots these aggregated measures. The box starts at the first quartile and ends at the third quartile. This range in the box is the interquartile range (half of the values). The line inside the box represents the median value. The lines outside the box, called the whiskers, branch out to the lowest value (the minimum) and the highest value (the maximum). A box plot for our data is represented in Figure 1b.

Tufte (1983) suggests another version of Tukey's box plot which is depicted in Figure 1c. If you look carefully you can see that this plot, called a *line plot*, represents the same statistical measures as the box plot but the box is missing. The median is represented by a dot. The whitespace between the lines and the dot represents the interquartile range. Obviously you need to be keenly aware of what these aggregate measures mean before you can start interpreting Tukey's and Tufte's plots.

Let us now move on to the visualization of frequency tables. You will recall from the previous chapter that frequency tables are special kinds of summary tables, in that they provide aggregate measures for one variable. Table 5.11 on page 77 gave an example for the derived attribute Revenue.

The type of chart you choose for the visualization of these frequency tables depends on the measurement scale of your variable. If you have a frequency table for an ordinal, interval, or ratio-scaled variable, you would use a *histogram*. Figure 2 displays a histogram for Table 5.11.

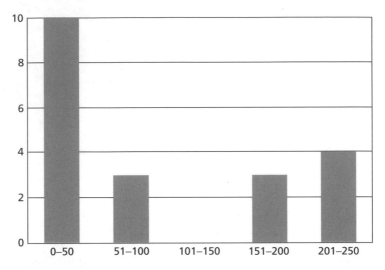

Figure 2 Histogram

A histogram has two axes, a horizontal axis representing the bins, and a vertical axis representing the frequency.

If you are visualizing a nominal-scaled variable, you would use a *bar chart* to represent your frequency table. A bar chart is like a histogram but the nominal values do not represent any order. To avoid confusion with the histogram, the bar chart is often depicted horizontally. Figure 3 gives an example of a bar chart, depicting the number of times each sales agent has secured a sales order.

If we are more interested in the relative frequency, rather than absolute frequency, we can visualize a variable with a *pie chart* or a *stacked bar chart*. You would use these charts to emphasize the percentages, not the absolute data values. Figure 4 gives an example of both types of charts. You can see that the stacked bar chart is simply a 'stretched out' version of the pie chart.

6.3. **Visualizing two variables**

The previous section discussed frequency tables and the different types of charts to visualize these. We can extend that discussion to the entire range of summary tables.

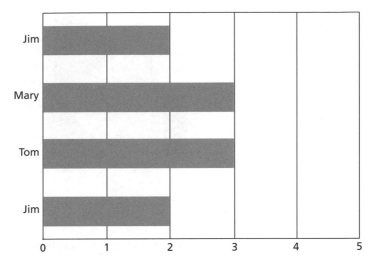

Figure 3 Bar chart

Summary tables, as we have seen in the previous chapter, provide aggregate data of one variable grouped by the values of another variable. The aggregated data is typically, although not necessarily all the time, on an interval or ratio-scale. The grouping variable is typically, although not necessarily all the time, on a nominal scale.

The summary table, just like the frequency table, is thus best visualized using bar charts and pie charts. The bar chart emphasizes absolute frequencies. The pie chart and stacked bar chart emphasizes relative frequencies. Figure 5 gives an example for the summary table from Table 5.9 on page 76. Note that I drew the bar chart upright here because the grouping

Figure 4 Pie chart and stacked bar chart

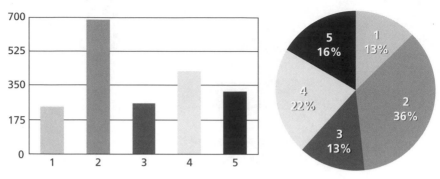

Figure 5 Visualization of summary tables

variable, week number, is an interval variable, and so a chart that resembles a histogram is more suitable.

Having visualized summary tables, we can now move on to cross-tabulations and pivot tables. Cross-tabulations, as you will recall from the previous chapter, are two summary tables split into a two-by-two matrix. Thus, they represent the same aggregated values, broken down in two separate dimensions.

The typical way to visualize cross-tabulations is to use the *side-by-side* variants of the univariate charts that we have discussed. Figure 6 illustrates four ways of doing this. The original data for these four charts is in Table 5.12 on p. 78.

The top left chart collates the sales agents together and orders them by week. The top right chart collates the weeks together and orders them by sales agent. Both charts are side-by-side bar charts. They focus on the absolute values. Which variable you collate is largely arbitrary, and depends on your preferences to examine the data.

The bottom two charts are side-by-side versions of the stacked bar chart. Here, the focus is on the relative frequencies. Please study all four visualizations of the base data from Table 5.12 carefully.

When using a side-by-side variant of a chart, you will need to use different colours or patterns to identify the different categories. You therefore need to include a legend, to show which colour or pattern you have assigned to which value.

Side-by-side variants of univariate charts should be contrasted to *bivariate charts*, which aim to visualize *a relationship* between one variable and

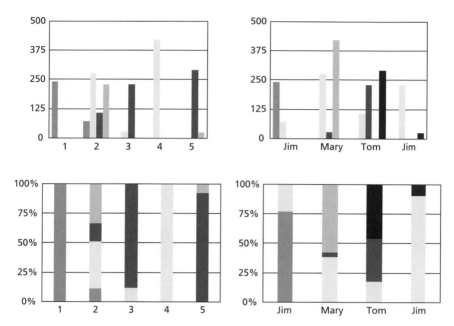

Figure 6 Visualizations of sample cross tab from Table 5.12 on p. 78

another. The technical name for what we are visualizing is *co-variation* because we are attempting to detect whether the variables change 'together', or in other words: whether a change in one variable is accompanied by a change in another. If that is the case, we would say that the variables 'co-vary'. Bivariate charts are nearly always about two interval- or ratio-scaled variables. To see whether nominal or ordinal variables co-vary, you would typically resort to the side-by-side variants.

Bivariate charts map the scales of the first variable and the second variable onto two axes, one horizontal (the *X*-axis) and one vertical (the *Y*-axis). By common convention the scaling is not distorted, that is, a range on the axis represents an equal range on the scale. There are some important deviations from this convention (notably logarithmic scaling) but for management purposes these are seldom used, and I shall ignore them here.

When constructing bivariate charts it is often possible to declare one variable as the independent variable, and the other attribute as the dependent variable. The *independent variable* is the variable that represents the

Table 6.1 Sample multivariate data

Entity	Var1	Var2	Var3	Var4
1	60	21	40	8
2	35	8	33	5
3	78	30	60	14
4	71	15	51	10
5	53	17	43	10
6	57	9	35	6
7	25	3	25	7
8	45	13	38	11
9	49	18	43	13
10	43	13	29	8
11	39	7	32	7
12	51	7	35	5
13	44	8	35	5
14	75	17	54	18
15	38	8	46	9
16	83	29	49	13
17	60	16	52	12
18	41	4	27	5
19	40	13	35	7
20	58	11	47	8

cause. The *dependent variable* is the variable that represents the effect. Doing so defines the direction of co-variation. If you assign variable A as independent and variable B as dependent, you are assuming that a change in A will lead to a change in B, but not the other way around. Declaring a dependency has important implications for the chart because the independent variable should go on the horizontal axis, and the dependent variable should go on the vertical axis.

You should be aware that proclaiming a dependency between variables (i.e. setting one as the independent and the other as the dependent) does not mean that this is actually the case. Sometimes the data may falsely suggest a dependency relationship, leading you to believe that there is a dependency but in fact there is none. Under such false belief you may well create misleading charts.

The opportunities to draw bivariate charts from the tables that we have seen in the previous chapter are rather limited because there are not too many interval and ratio variables to examine. Let us therefore examine a second result set, Table 6.1. This is a fictitious result set displaying 4

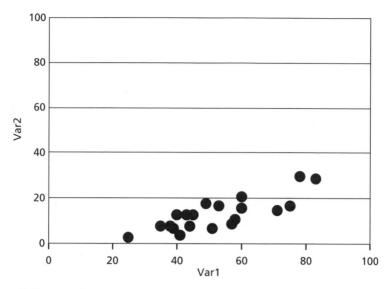

Figure 7 Scatter plot

variables about 20 entities. Because we are dealing with two variables at present, let us focus on Var1 and Var2 only.

The *scatter plot* is the bivariate extension of the dot scale, with each dot representing two values, one on the X-axis, and the other on the Y-axis. Note that charting a scatter plot does not imply that the variables co-vary, or that they share a dependency relationship. It is rather the purpose of drawing a scatter plot to explore the two variables, to see whether a co-variation can be suspected. Figure 7 draws the scatter plot for Var1 and Var2. You can see that the scatterplot suggests a linear covariation between the two variables: higher values of Var1 are associated with higher values of Var2.

When two variables co-vary, the dependency relationship can be there, but there are three other possibilities. First of all, that dependency may be suggested but non-existent, in that a change in one variable does not actually lead to a change in another, but is rather the result of pure coincidence. Second, the direction of the dependency may be the other way around. The third possibility, often overlooked, is that the variables may change together as a result of a change in a third variable, the *spurious* variable. The spurious variable is perhaps not even modelled, and it may be difficult to locate it.

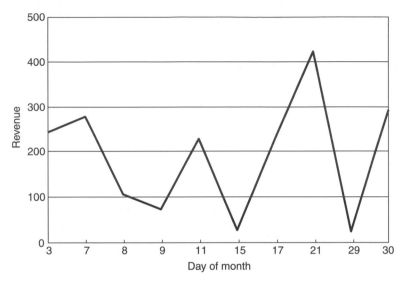

Figure 8 Line chart

In sum, if you are studying the relationships between two variables, do not assign a dependency relationship lightly. Think carefully about the other three options, and if you are unsure, be careful not to assign one. If you are in doubt, the measurement scale of the variables might be of help. Nominal data is often (but not always) independent. Time series variables are also often (but not always) independent.

The final chart to be discussed in this section is the *line chart*. The line chart is a special kind of scatter plot, where a line is then drawn between the points. The line suggests a trend, and it suggests that the values on the line can be inferred.

A special kind of line chart is the time series chart, which uses a time series variable to display on its *X*-axis and some other variable (often one that is ordinal and up) to display on its *Y*-axis. Figure 8 represents such a line chart. It plots the revenue from our previous chapter on a time line.

6.4. **Visualizing three or more variables**

When we need to visualize three variables at the same time, we have a number of options. First, we can use a three-dimensional (3D) scatter plot

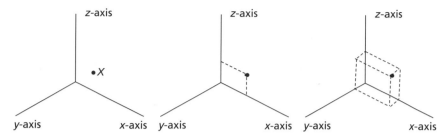

Figure 9 3D scatter plot

or 3D line chart, using an X-axis, a Y-axis, and a Z-axis. We can then plot our values in a three-dimensional space. This is not without problems though, because the exact data values on the X, Y, and Z axes are often ambiguous. See, for example, Figure 9 and you will note that the location of point X is ambiguous without the auxiliary dotted lines.

Imagine I had to visualize Var1, Var2, and Var3 from Table 6.1. I could map them on three axes and create a 3D line plot. This would create much confusion because each point would be subject to the same ambiguity that affected Figure 9. A better alternative, that only works with three variables, is to create a *bubble chart*. A bubble chart is like a bivariate scatter plot, but the values on the third dimension are represented by the width of the dot (effectively turning the dot into a bubble). I have demonstrated this in Figure 10.

Looking at patterns in bubble charts, we need to look for co-varation again. Larger-sized bubbles (higher values of Var3) would seem to be asso ciated with higher values of Var1 and higher values of Var2. It would thus seem that there is a positive co-variation between all three variables.

One other option for three-dimensional data, frequently used, is to simplify the visualization by plotting out all possible *two-dimensional* relationships in a *scatter plot matrix*. If we want to visualize three dimensions, we would need $3 \times 2 \times 1 = 6$ two-dimensional plots. Figure 11 shows how this would work. We could this do for tables with ever higher dimensions, but the number of two-dimensional scatterplots will rise exponentially.

To visualize four dimensions, we could resort to the bubble chart again. That is because we could map the fourth dimension onto a colour gradient (e.g. shades of blue) and colour the bubbles in the bubble chart with their respective value to represent the fourth variable. The problem with these

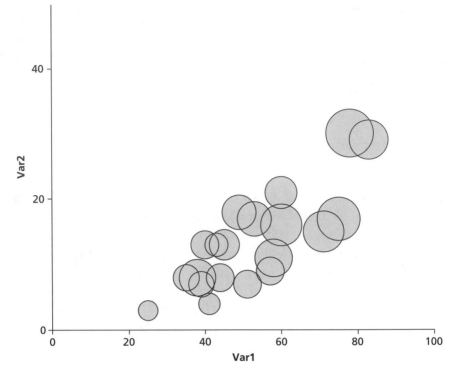

Figure 10 Bubble chart

coloured bubble-charts is that it is becoming increasingly difficult to see the relationships between the relevant dimensions. Are higher values of Var1 associated with higher values of Var2 and with larger bubbles and with darker bubbles? Do all four variables co-vary with each other?

Multi-dimensional data with five or more dimensions are even harder to visualize, and few techniques are available to do so effectively. The most common way is to use a *parallel coordination plot*. With such a plot, you put the axes parallel to each other (one for each variable), and for each instance you draw a line to connect the individual values on each of the axes. For example, let us look at the first four instances of Table 6.1. I have drawn these values into the parallel coordination plot from Figure 12.

Sometimes the axes are not put in parallel but rather in circular format, resulting in something that is called a *radar chart* or *star plot*. Figure 13 gives an example of the same data, this time in a radar chart.

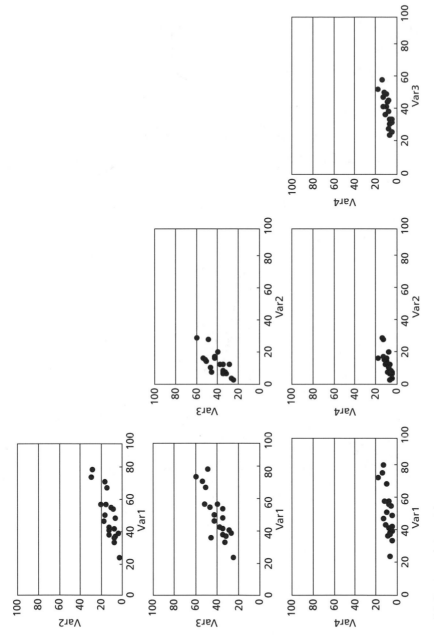

Figure 11 Scatter plot matrix

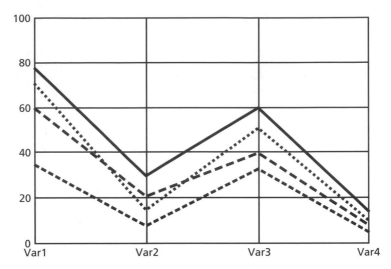

Figure 12 Parallel coordination plot

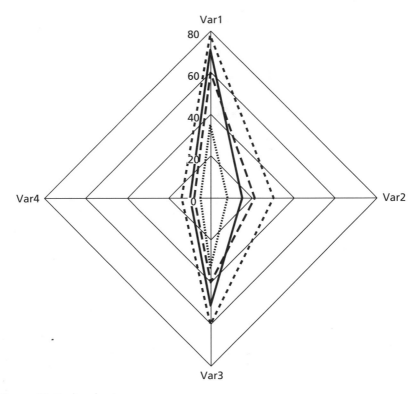

Figure 13 Radar chart

These plots are also not without serious problems. For a start, parallel coordination plots are often confused with line charts. Second, the plot becomes very cluttered quickly with more than four or five instances. If I had mapped out all 20 instances from Table 6.1 in Figure 12, it would be impossible to identify any pattern at all.

A further limitation of these plots is that they only really work well with variables that are measured on exactly the same scale. It is perhaps tempting to put axes next to each other that are from different scales (e.g. ordinal or even nominal), but in that case the choice of axes and the choice of the position of the values can seriously distort the overall picture. Standardization of interval and ratio scales works, but it would require conversion and transformation of data, which is not generally helpful to understand the data better.

A number of other multidimensional visualization techniques do exist but they are not very widely used. *Chernoff faces* deserve special mention (Chernoff 1973), because they can represent entities on no less than 18 dimensions, using facial features such as ear size, distance between eyes, and so on.

It can be argued that in our three-dimensional world we simply find it very difficult to understand data with more than three dimensions. If we have to face up to that reality, we must also realize that we will probably never find a good way of visualizing data with more than three dimensions.

I should complete this section with mentioning two statistical techniques that compress multidimensional data into data with fewer dimensions. *Factor analysis* can reduce dimensions by creating a so-called factor score: one value that represents the values on all four or more dimensions. *Cluster analysis* reduces the instances by creating clusters of instances: one instance that represents instances with similar values on their dimensions.

The aggregate values that cluster and factor analyses produce can help us to visualize the data more effectively, particularly when we enter four or more dimensions. For example, a cluster analysis can cluster the 20 instances from Table 6.1 into, say, 4 clusters, which could then be effectively represented on a parallel coordination plot. A discussion of factor and cluster analysis is beyond the scope of this book but I encourage you to study them in greater detail.

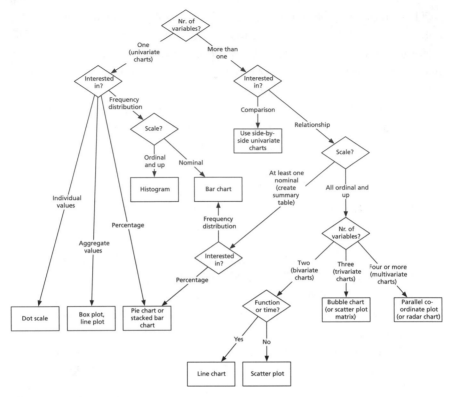

Figure 14 Chart pointer

I have summarized the visualization possibilities in a decision tree (Figure 14). You can use this tree to check which chart is best suited for which purpose.

6.5. Dynamic charts

Dynamic charts are charts that change in appearance after a user interaction. They are a powerful way of visualizing trends, and they can also save screen space in that they can replace a series of static charts. By definition, dynamic charts can only be implemented in computerized information systems, and they cannot be used in traditional management reports.

In this section I will discuss several examples. The first technique is called *brushing*, first described by Becker and Cleveland (1987). The technique makes use of the mouse. You use the mouse to point at a certain dot, or area, in the chart and the chart changes shape as a result of you pointing at that dot. For example, in Figure 9, you can point at a particular dot in one scatter plot, and the system can highlight dots from the same instance in all other scatter plots. Another example is to move the 'brush' over a time series, and the chart will display some detailed information about the time that is at the location of the mouse pointer.

The second example is to use what might be called an *interactive legend*. If there are too many entities or category values to display, you can use a legend that is interactive. Each of the category values can be turned on or turned off. In a parallel coordination plot, for example, you would be able to turn on or off the lines of specific instances to focus on just the ones you want to highlight.

An interactive legend is actually a specific example of a more general technique called *overlays*. The overlay technique first organizes the tables and charts into layers, and then allows you to turn on or off the display of each layer. One layer can be superimposed over another layer to add information. Layers can also be taken away so that less information is presented.

Think of overlays as using transparencies on a traditional data projector, for example, to display information about a country. Your first transparency would be the outline of a country. Your next transparency could be the same outline of the country, but this time with coloured areas, with each colour depicting a language that is spoken in that area. The next transparency could show where the mountainous areas are. You can flip between the language and mountain transparencies if you want, so that the language data will not distract from the mountain data.

Although you can imagine applying overlays using a traditional data projector, the technique comes to full bloom using an interactive user interface. So, in a computerized version of the above example, you could have two buttons next to the country chart, called 'Display languages' and 'Display mountains', which would allow you to toggle the language and the mountain layers.

Overlays can be used in geographical maps but also in charts such as the one we saw in Figure 8. An information system applying this technique would allow you to select just the sales agent (or team) that you want to see in the chart. If you combine it with aggregation measures, it can show you, for example, the average sales revenue as well. This then would allow you to see how an individual sales agent, say Jim, is doing in comparison to the average.

6.6. **Colour and other visual effects**

Applying colour to your management information can have three powerful effects. First of all, there is the informational effect. Colour can be used to add information to a chart. For example, it can be used to indicate 'good' and 'bad' values on a chart by colouring the values green and red, respectively. A colour gradient (e.g. light blue to dark blue) might be mapped to the values of a variable, and you can then use colour to represent the values of the variable. We have discussed how such an effect might be useful to represent four dimensions in a bubble chart.

The second effect is the isolation effect. A colour can be used to isolate a certain data value from the others, thereby drawing attention to that particular data value. Of course this effect only works if you use colours very sparsely. If too many colours compete for attention, then eventually the isolation effect is destroyed.

The third effect pursued by adding colour is to produce aesthetic effects. The aesthetic effect that colours produce is often called *colour harmony*. The harmony is the result of a combination of colours that gives a sense of visual order and balance.

Choosing a colour can produce all three effects at the same time, so this exercise should be taken very seriously. One way to select a colour is to use a 'colour wheel'. Such a wheel displays a number of colours adjacent to each other, forming a circle. To achieve a harmonious effect, you can then choose colours that are analogous to each other, that is, right next to each other on the colour wheel. To achieve a contrasting effect, you can choose colours that are complementary to each other, that is, that are on opposite ends of each other on the colour wheel. Yet there are no hard and fast rules and choosing colours remains somewhat of an art. I have found the book of Albers (2006) worth reading for inspiration.

Which ever colours you choose in the end, do not use too many and use them conservatively. I would recommend not more than three or four. The reason is that the three effects described above start to compete with each other quickly when you add more colours, and you will quickly confuse the reader as to which effect you actually wanted to achieve. Also, any aesthetic effect is easily destroyed by too many colours: they will quickly turn into disharmony.

The topic of colours brings me to the final point I would like to make in this chapter. Most commercial management information systems allow you to 'dress up' your charts: not just with colours but also with shadow effects, beautiful backgrounds, and so on. Particularly notorious is the 3D effect, which adds a (fake) dimension of depth to otherwise two-dimensional bars and pie charts. For some reason information system designers (and managers) find such effects irresistibly attractive.

Avoid using them, for two important reasons. The first reason is that these effects often distort the correct presentation of data, particularly when it comes to representing proportions. Consider for example Figure 15. The figure displays two pie charts, both representing the same data.

The 3D version admittedly looks much better. But you will note that the values for B and E are particularly distorted in the 3D version. The 2D

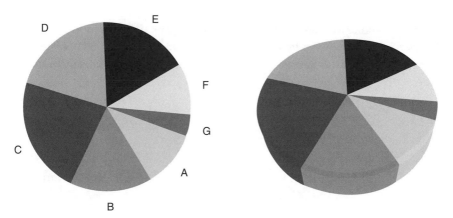

Figure 15 2D and 3D pie charts

version visualizes (correctly) that the value for E is larger than the value for B. The 3D version appears to suggest (incorrectly) that the value for B is larger than the value for E.

The second reason not to dress up your chart is that the chart itself will start to attract more attention than the data that provided the basis for the chart. In more dramatic terms: the more visual effects you add, the more you suffocate the original data. This is sending out the wrong signal to the recipient of the information. Why is the chart itself so important? Are you not convinced yourself that the data is worthy of study?

☐ FURTHER READING

There is a sizable body of literature dealing with visualization of data. I would recommend starting with Tukey's classic Exploratory Data Analysis (1977). Tukey introduces the box plot here, as well as a range of other techniques. After reading Tukey I would suggest studying Cleveland's books (1985 1993).

More recent books on information visualization include Ware (2004) and Spence (2007). Also popular are Tufte's books, and I would particularly recommend his first one on the visual display of quantitative information (1983). Few's book on designing information dashboards is also well worth reading (Few 2006). All these books offer, as you would expect, beautiful (and somewhat esoteric) visualizations of data.

I talked in this chapter about the danger of misrepresenting data, for example, by suggesting a dependency relationship when in fact there is none. Huff (1991) gives a number of very good examples in his well-known book on *How to lie with statistics*.

Good examples of charts can be found in books by Wildbur and Burke (1998) and Harris (1999). A fine example can also be found in an article by Powsner and Tufte (1994), which contains a graphical summary of medical information of a patient.

Part II

Supporting Management Decisions

7 Monitoring key performance indicators

KEY THEMES

When you have read this chapter, you should be able to define those key concepts in your own words, and you should also be able to:

1. Identify key performance indicators for a set of managerial entities.
2. Organize and group these performance indicators in a variety of frameworks.
3. Outline a range of techniques to understand the variability of these performance indicators.

7.1. Introduction

As a manager you will spend a substantial portion of your time studying the performance of entities and relationships, and invoke some corrective action in case that performance falls below certain thresholds. Under these circumstances it is often helpful if a management information system not only displays the performance itself but also the changes in performance over time. In addition, a management information system can alert a manager as soon as performance changes unexpectedly. On the basis of such an alert, one could then decide whether such corrective action is required.

Monitoring a select set of vital indicators of performance is the type of management decision that we are concerned with in this chapter. It is common to refer to these indicators as *key performance indicators*, or *KPIs*. I will start this chapter with an overview of various frameworks to organize and arrange key performance indicators.

The rest of the chapter then discusses four particular techniques that management information systems can employ to support the monitoring of key performance indicators. These techniques either involve 'upgraded' visualization techniques, especially relevant to monitor KPIs, or they involve interactive functionality that can help in identifying unexpected variability in performance.

A common theme with these techniques is the *variability* of the indicator. Variability of an indicator is a measure of the extent to which an indicator is subject to changes. Variability can be more or less predictable. If we cannot entirely predict the variability of the indicator, we would call the KPI a *stochastic* variable. Managerial KPIs are often stochastic because they depend on customer demand, which is difficult to predict. The opposite of a stochastic variable is a *deterministic* variable. The techniques that we discuss in this chapter are to help the manager find out the nature of the stochastic process, and whether there is a need to take action.

7.2. Identifying key performance indicators

The first thing that we would like a management information system to do is to display key performance indicators in a single, concise, high-level, summary report. We often refer to such a management report as a *scorecard*. Just like we would write the scores of a football match onto a scorecard, so would we enter the 'scores' of a company on a scorecard.

A related term that has recently become popular is the *information dashboard* (Few 2006), or simply *dashboard*. The term is often used to mean an 'interactive scorecard', that is, a scorecard that is equipped with interactive functionality to modify the display of the KPIs on the scorecard.

The question now becomes: what key performance indicators should go on the scorecard? Identifying and selecting good indicators is an important part of the design of the management information system. It requires you to think hard about the way the entities are being managed.

One way to start this exercise is to look at the measures that say something about the 'health' of the entities and the relationships that we are managing. For example, if we are managing a sales organization, an indicator that reflects the health of the sales organization could be the total sales revenue in a particular month.

A second way to start the exercise is to look at the entity life cycle, and look at the various stages that an entity can be in. We could then study the 'rites of passage' for each stage, and identify indicators that tell us how many instances went from one stage to the next. Conversion rates (e.g. converting promising leads into prospects, and converting prospects into customers) are examples of indicators that can come up using this approach.

The identification of key performance indicators can draw inspiration from the long-term strategy that the manager or management team has identified. It is not uncommon in organizations to link key performance indicators directly to strategic directions. For example, if our strategic direction is to grow market share for certain products, then a key performance indicator will be share of total sales revenue compared to total market sales. If our long-term strategy is to grow revenue in non-food products at the expense of food-related products, then a key performance indicator will be the proportion of non-food products that forms part of our total sales revenue.

Identifying a connection with long-term strategy is often much more difficult than it sounds. For a start, the strategy may not be very explicit. It may also not have been very recently updated. Finally, the long-term strategy may not be sufficiently expressive, in that it is at too high a level to derive meaningful KPIs from. In those cases, MIS designers will often find themselves second-guessing strategic directions.

In identifying key performance indicators for scorecards, you do not need to start from scratch. There are a wide range of existing templates at our disposal. The grandfather of them all is the template introduced by Kaplan and Norton in 1996: the *Balanced Scorecard*, or *BSC* (Kaplan and Norton 1996).

I should point out immediately that this is a scorecard for a standard, profit-maximizing, company. If we want to monitor something else, for example an organization that does not necessarily aim to maximize profits such as a charity, we need to modify the scorecard or perhaps invent a totally new one.

What is balanced about the balanced scorecard is that it does not solely focus on financial performance indicators, such as sales revenue and profits. Kaplan and Norton argue that these financial figures are just one side of the company, or in their own words, one 'perspective'. The balanced scorecard identifies three other perspectives, each of which has its own set of key performance indicators. Here are all four of them:

Financial perspective: This is the 'traditional' perspective from the accounting point of view. It includes financial aggregated data that we can normally find on the balance sheet (assets and liabilities) and the profit and loss statement (income and expenses).

Ratios that can be grouped under this perspective include return on investment (income derived from investments divided by total cost of the investment).

Customer perspective: This is the perspective that one would take from a marketing point of view. It looks at performance indicators that a customer would find important. An example would be average delivery time of a product. This perspective also looks at performance indicators that refer to customers, such as customer satisfaction.

Ratios that can be grouped under this perspective include the so-called 'conversion' ratios (e.g. percentage of prospects that actually end up being customers).

Internal business process perspective: This is the perspective dealing with the management of operations. Key performance indicators may include inventory stock levels, or the time that it takes to finish assembling products.

Learning and growth perspective: This is the perspective dealing with human resource management. It can include ratios such as employee turnover and so on, as well as specific indicators related to staff development.

The BSC is normally presented as a one-page summary report with the perspectives symmetrically arranged for aesthetic effect. Figure 1 provides an example.

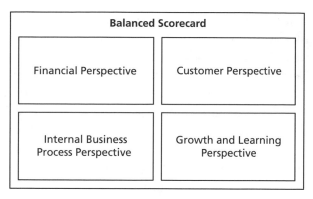

Figure 1 The balanced scorecard

This framework is certainly not the only framework to cluster key performance indicators. The influential management thinker Peter Drucker has offered another one. In his paper on 'the information that managers truly need' (Drucker 1995), he identifies the following types of key performance indicators:

Foundation information: This, according to Drucker, is straightforward diagnostic information of the entities and relationships that we are managing. An example is the revenue that sales teams are generating.

Productivity information: This is diagnostic information that tells us something about the productivity of the entities and relationships that we are managing. An example, is the average sales revenue for a sales agent.

Competence information: This is diagnostic information about the performance of the competencies that the organization is particularly good at. In a way this is the more strategic side of foundation information, focusing on the long-term strategic directions of the company.

Resource allocation information: This is diagnostic information about the way resources are allocated and the efficiency with which this takes place.

The categorizations of Kaplan, Norton, and Drucker can provide suitable starting points to identify the key performance indicators for your management information system.

Once you have identified your key performance indicators, it is useful to distinguish between lagging and leading indicators. *Lagging indicators* are indicators of events that have happened in the past. For example, sales volume is a lagging indicator because it tells us something about the success of sales transactions that have occurred in the past. *Leading indicators* are indicators of events that will happen in the future. For example, the number of current prospects is a leading indicator because it tells us something about the success of sales transactions that will occur in the future. Indicators can both be leading and lagging. The number of current prospects, for example, is also a lagging indicator of how successful we were in converting promising leads into prospects.

Finally, the key performance indicators can be organized into hierarchies. Indicators at a lower level (e.g. sales volume from sales team Alpha) can then feed into indicators at a higher level (e.g. sales volume from all teams). Advanced business intelligence systems allow you to define high-level strategic objectives (such as 'increase conversion ratios') and then group the relevant indicators that you would need to see if your objective is being met into a lower level of the hierarchy. It is then possible to drill down from strategic objectives to lower-level indicators.

7.3. **Adding bandwidth**

A key performance indicator is typically conceptualized as an aggregated data value, and often a derived one. We can visualize KPIs according to the principles discussed in Chapter 6. I have little to contribute to that chapter with respect to key performance indicators, and so we will not revisit that material here.

Performance indicators are often tracked over time because it is often not so much the value of a KPI itself, but rather its variability that is of importance. Such a study of a KPI over time is called a *trend analysis*. To study trends we need to look at the changes of the KPI over time. For this reason, the visualization often takes the form of a time series chart.

To aid the interpretation of such a chart, it can be helpful to include a *bandwidth*. Figure 2 gives an example of adding such a bandwidth.

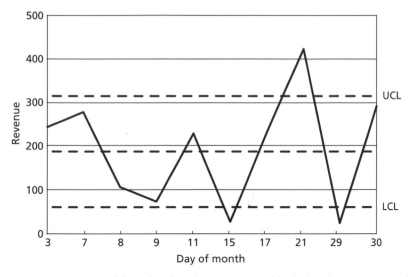

Figure 2 Lower control limit (LCL) and upper control limit (UCL)

Figure 2 shows a normal time series chart, similar to the one in Chapter 6 from page 90 but with three extra lines representing a band. The middle line is the average for the 12 months. It is sometimes called the *centre line*, or the process average. The lower and upper lines refer to the *lower control limit* (LCL) and *upper control limit* (UCL), respectively. A time series chart that has such a band is also often called a *process chart*.

How do we set the bandwidth? We need to define or calculate the LCL and UCL. A common way to do it is to look at the mean and the standard deviation of the KPI over a certain time period. A limit is then usually set at the mean plus or minus three times the standard deviation. Anything that is above or below three times the standard deviation is statistically an outlier. This is the method that we have used in Figure 2.

Figure 2 displays a *stable* bandwidth. We call it a stable bandwidth because it does not co-vary with the value of the KPI. It is also possible to define a band that changes as the KPI itself changes. These are called *dynamic* bandwidths. For example, rather than defining limits using a stable average over a fixed period of time, we can recalculate the limits based on 'moving averages', that is, averages that are updated with the latest KPI values. Such moving averages are often used in stock exchange data to track the variability of stock prices.

The idea behind adding a bandwidth is that there will always be some stochastic variability in the key performance indicator, but it need not be substantial until it moves out of the margins that the LCL and UCL provide. The manager can then decide to take action only when the KPI is approaching or crossing the LCL and UCL.

An important advantage of adding a bandwidth is the ease with which we can spot extreme performance. For example, in Figure 2 we can see fairly quickly which days were very poor and which day was very good for this key performance indicator.

7.4. **Adding comparative indicators**

To appreciate the magnitude of a certain value of a performance indicator, that value is often compared to a related value. A management information system can perform those comparisons with a range of related values. Such a comparative analysis is often also called a *variance analysis* or difference analysis.

There are at least three types of comparative analysis that we can identify for any one KPI. I have listed them below.

Historical comparison: Here we compare the value of a KPI with a the value of that KPI in the past. For example, a value could be compared to the same value last week, last month, or last year.

Target comparison: Here we compare the value of a KPI with a value that we would like it to have, the so-called target level. The definition of the target can be set in advance, or it can be dynamic in that it changes as the KPI itself changes.

Competitive comparison: Here we compare the value of a KPI with a value that one or more competing organizations have managed to achieve.

With comparison analysis, the descriptive values are not so much of interest, but rather the degree to which the value has changed from a value in the past. For example, reporting that the stock levels of a company are 20 per cent up from last year is perhaps better than reporting last year you had 64 days and this year you had 76.8. If that difference is the subject of

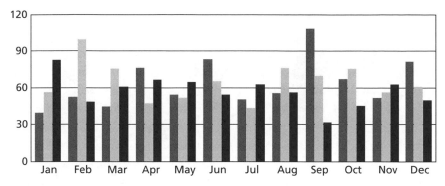

Figure 3 Competitive comparison between Alpha, Beta, and Gamma

interest, you can avoid information overload by reporting just the difference and not the two values that were used to calculate the difference.

The visualization of comparison, as we have seen in Chapter 6, is effectively performed with side-by-side versions of bar charts. For example, Figure 3 gives an example of competitive comparison between the three sales teams Alpha, Beta, and Gamma.

A second visualization that is often used is to display the comparative values together with the KPI in the process chart. We can then see how variability has developed in the comparative values, and how this would be different from the variability in the KPIs.

7.5. **Exceptions**

An important technique for reporting key performance indicators is called *exception*. In Figure 3, you saw how we could identify extreme values, those that were above the upper control limit or below the lower control limit. The idea behind the exception technique is to display the extreme data *only*. In using this technique, you would suppress the other data so that only the exceptions remain. Note how close this technique comes to Ackoff's principle of suppressing irrelevant information mentioned in Chapter 1.

To illustrate the dramatic effect of the technique, consider Tables 7.1 and 7.2. Table 7.1 displays a total of 84 values. Table 7.2 shows just the seven statistical outliers.

Table 7.1 A table with a fictitious data set

	Jan	Feb	Mar	Apr	May	Jun	Jul	Aug	Sep	Oct	Nov	Dec
A	40	53	45	77	55	84	51	56	109	68	52	82
B	57	100	76	48	52	66	44	77	70	76	57	61
C	83	49	61	67	65	55	63	57	32	46	63	50
D	72	43	59	38	61	57	50	28	77	51	19	56
E	63	65	35	16	57	100	94	46	103	63	47	68
F	36	61	55	16	60	82	62	61	38	57	64	84
G	15	77	81	80	52	66	65	30	45	41	53	61

If you are using the exception technique, you need to design criteria for values that are to be classified as extreme. In my example with the two tables, the statistical outliers of the data set are classified as exceptions. But aside from the statistical outliers, you could also have chosen extreme values based on other criteria. These include, for example, the best ranking unit in every month (resulting in 12 exceptions), or the month in which every unit performed the worst (resulting in 7 exceptions). If the data is part of a time series, as is the case here, the system could treat data that suddenly becomes highly volatile as exceptions.

Choosing the criteria that 'upgrades' a value to an extreme value is a balancing act where the information system designer faces a trade-off between the limited amount of user attention and the innate 'desire' for every value to be an exception. In case of doubt, you might consider leaving the definition of an exception to the user. For example, you can have the user set a threshold value, and if the value exceeds that threshold, the system should treat it as an extreme value and alert the user.

Table 7.2 Table 7.1 with extreme values only

	Jan	Feb	Mar	Apr	May	Jun	Jul	Aug	Sep	Oct	Nov	Dec
A									109			
B		100										
C												
D												
E				16		100			103			
F				16								
G	15											

In most spreadsheet software you can draw attention to extreme values by using a function called *conditional formatting*. You can specify a condition (e.g. the cell value is greater than 100), and have the cell formatted in a specific way if that condition is true (e.g. showing the extreme values in red). To hide all the values that do not represent exceptions, you can use conditional formatting too: choose as your condition all values that do not represent exceptions (e.g. all cell values less than 100), and format them such that their font colour is the same as their background colour (e.g. white on white). Only the extreme will remain visible.

7.6. **Sensitivity analysis**

A final technique to discuss in the context of monitoring key performance indicators is *sensitivity analysis*. A sensitivity analysis simulates the changes that can occur in a KPI if certain base data changes.

We have seen earlier that a KPI is often derived from base data. To calculate a KPI thus requires a number of input values. If these input values change, then so does the value of the KPI. For example, aggregated sales revenue is dependent on the number of sales orders that the sales organization manages to secure. A sensitivity analysis would display the effect of these changes on the value of the KPI. This type of sensitivity analysis is also commonly known as 'what-if' analysis.

It is common to think of the technique as 'tinkering' with input to examine the effect on output. But the analysis can also work the other way around: you can fix the value of the output and see what kind of input values you would need to arrive at that particular output. This type of analysis, where you manipulate the goal output to see how the input should change, is often called 'goal-seeking' analysis.

Sensitivity analysis is well developed in the field of mathematical programming, which studies problems where an optimal decision is calculated given certain input parameters. It is beyond the scope of this book to study these sensitivity analyses in more detail, and I will have to refer to more specialized material on the subject.

Although researchers have put substantial effort into the mathematics of sensitivity analyses, research into the visualization of these analyses has

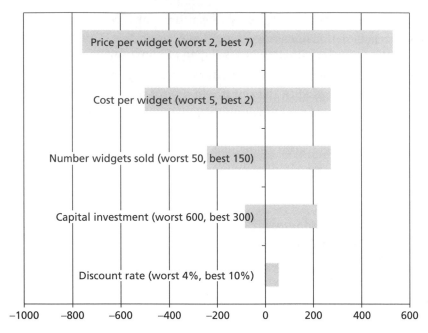

Figure 4 Tornado chart

not been as forthcoming. It appears to be difficult to convey a picture of a sensitivity analysis. The only chart that I am aware of that captures sensitivity analysis graphically is the so-called *tornado chart*.

An example of a tornado chart is provided in Figure 4. I have used a simple example where I calculate the cost of a project in which I will produce and sell 'widgets'. The five input parameters that I use in my net present value calculation are price per widget, cost per widget, capital investment, and the discount rate. The tornado chart represents the sensitivity in net present value for five input parameters. The horizontal axis represents the *change* in KPI if I vary the value of each of these input parameters.

The sensitivity analysis for this tornado chart uses three values for every input parameter: a worst-case value, a best-case value, and a base-case value. The bar for each input parameter represents the difference in the KPI ranging from worst-case to best-case (with the base case 0). Sensitivity is measured as the length of the interval between the KPI between worst and best case. A tornado chart sorts the bars according to their sensitivity, that is, the ones that are the most sensitive come on top.

How should you interpret a tornado chart? The tornado chart provides you an overview of the impact of your confidence on the eventual outcome of the result. So, in this case, it tells you that the price per widget is going to have the biggest impact on the KPI. The discount rate is going to have the lowest impact on my KPI. Price per widget is thus the most sensitive input parameter: I need to look very carefully at this parameter, that is, see if I can improve confidence in my base case value by decreasing the range within which it can vary. Discount rate is the least sensitive input parameter: it does not really matter what value it has (within the range I have specified), because it is not going to have such a big impact.

Tornado charts are not yet supported in the mainstream spreadsheet packages, which is unfortunate because there are very few techniques that visualize sensitivity in performance indicators. The other alternative is dynamic charts, in which one can vary an input parameter with (say) a slider bar, and one can immediately witness the effect on the performance indicator in (say) a bar chart. Professional business intelligence packages use dynamic charts to very good effect, and it is worth the effort to spend time studying the options that are available if you have access to such tools.

□ **FURTHER READING**

In this chapter I have focused on management decisions that arise from monitoring key performance indicators. I have discussed several frameworks to organize KPIs, and I have outlined four techniques that an MIS designer can use to assist a manager in these decisions. Let me summarize these techniques here.

The first technique involves the introduction of the 'bandwidth'. This technique allows the manager to examine whether the variability of a KPI is within certain safety margins.

The second technique is the addition of comparative indicators. The performance of a particular KPI is often judged in comparison with the performance of that KPI in a previous period. This technique allows the manager to examine whether the variability of a KPI is in line with one that could be expected from previous periods.

The third technique is the introduction of exception management. With this technique, the information system keeps track of certain threshold values for performance indicators, and will alert the manager if the performance is either above or below those thresholds.

The final technique discussed in this chapter is sensitivity analysis. This technique simulates the effects of certain changes on the performance of the key indicator. It gives the manager an insight in the patterns that can occur as the KPI varies.

For further reading, I would recommend studying a range of balanced scorecards and information dashboards, such as the ones provided in Kaplan, Norton, and Few (2006).

8 Selecting alternatives

KEY CONCEPTS

Decision matrix

Decision strategy

Alternative or attribute-based decisions

Compensatory or non-compensatory
  decisions

Consideration set

Effort–accuracy trade-off

Shortlist

Utility mapping

KEY THEMES

When you have read this chapter, you should be able to define those key concepts in your own words, and you should also be able to:

1. Apply the different decision strategies.

2. Understand the importance of the consideration set.

3. Outline a range of techniques to assist in choosing an alternative from a list of many available options.

8.1. Introduction

This chapter covers a second class of decisions that managers frequently have to make: selecting the most appropriate alternative out of a list of alternatives. We will discuss this particular type of decision in more detail and then focus on the ways that management information systems can help to support these types of decisions.

There are many examples of these types of decisions. Typical ones include the selection of an appropriate supplier of a certain material or service, or the selection of an appropriate candidate out of a list of suitable candidates for a particular vacancy.

The available alternatives in these examples have a common set of attributes. Suppliers list materials by type, price, delivery date, discount opportunities, and so on. Candidates can be listed by name, experience, employment history, references, and so on. These types of decisions are often called *preferential choice tasks*, because the decision-maker is faced with the task of choosing the best alternative that matches his or her preferences.

This type of decision is fortunate enough to have enjoyed a good deal of academic research. Psychologists have made much progress in understanding this type of decision-making, and I will make frequent use of their findings in this chapter.

This chapter is organized as follows: I will first discuss the general structure of these decisions and outline the strategies that we have available to tackle them. I will then move on to discuss the implications for information system designers. The next sections will again discuss a number of techniques that information systems designers can use. I will end the chapter with a summary.

8.2. **The decision matrix**

To start off this chapter, it is useful to have a look at a more detailed example of the type of decisions that we are dealing with here. Suppose you need to select a vendor for a particular material, say wood, to be used in your production process. For your convenience I have compiled 12 possible alternatives and presented them in Table 8.1. How would you approach such a decision, and which supplier would you eventually select?

Table 8.1 Search and select the best supplier

#	Region	Quality	Distance to plant	Distance to warehouse	Price
1	A	2 star	60	100	120
2	B	3 star	40	130	100
3	B	4 star	100	150	200
4	A	2 star	400	110	70
5	B	3 star	50	100	150
6	A	4 star	50	140	100
7	B	2 star	200	50	40
8	A	4 star	100	110	40
9	A	2 star	300	100	30
10	B	3 star	400	110	70
11	A	2 star	200	75	80
12	A	2 star	300	110	50

One thing that will immediately be clear from Table 8.1 is how similar the representation of the alternatives is to the de-normalized tables that we have been constructing at the end of Chapter 4. This is no coincidence. The construction of the decision matrix follows the same fundamental principles of structuring data as we have been discussing in Chapters 2 and 3. 'Hidden' in Table 8.1, for example, are the entities Supplier, Material, Region, and Quality Rating. I leave it as an exercise for you to construct the entity relationship diagram for this table.

A management information system should be able to display a decision matrix like Table 8.1 in an easy-to-read format, and allow users to manipulate rows (alternatives) and columns (attributes). Spreadsheets provide a range of functionalities to allow you to do this.

A second thing to notice from Table 8.1 is that we should again be focusing on opportunities to sort alternatives by attribute, and that the possibilities for ranking are again limited by the scale of the attribute. For example, region is a nominal scale and cannot as such be ranked. We cannot say that region A is 'higher' or 'lower' than region B. Note that you may have subjective preferences for particular regions and that your preference for region A may be 'higher', or 'lower' than your preference for region B. I shall return to this point later in this chapter. For now I leave it as another exercise for you to determine the scales of the other variables.

In case we are dealing with alternatives that have prices associated with them, it is common to display the price as the last attribute at the very end. I suspect this is because it makes it easier for the decision-maker to separate costs and benefits. All attributes except the last one make up the total package of 'benefits' which can then be offset against the last attribute which represents the 'cost'.

8.3. **Decision strategies**

Deciding on the best alternative in a decision matrix like Table 8.1 involves making many comparisons. Let us start by looking at the decision matrix and focusing in on a particular attribute value. For example, the price of wood from supplier #2: 100. To understand if that value is 'good' or 'bad' you will be making two types of comparisons. The first comparison centres on the *attribute*: you will look at the prices of other suppliers and see if they are cheaper or more expensive. It is a vertical, or column-based comparison. The other comparison centres on the *alternative*: you will look at the other values of this particular supplier and offset it against the price. It is a horizontal, or row-based comparison.

People apply a number of different approaches to solve a multi-attribute, multi-alternative decision problem. These approaches are often referred to as *decision strategies*. An extensive overview of possible decision strategies can be found in Svenson (1979).

Strategies can involve so-called pairwise comparisons. That means that you look at alternatives in pairs, compare them, and then discard the one that you do not like. For example, you can start off by comparing supplier #1 to supplier #2. You decide which one is the best, say supplier #1. You then move on supplier #3, and compare it with supplier #1. Now, let us say supplier #3 is the best. Supplier #3 then replaces supplier #1 as the best supplier so far. You then move on to supplier #4, and compare it with supplier #3. The process continues until you have reached the end of the list.

Let us look at eight common decision strategies (taken from a book by J. Payne, Bettman, and Johnson 1993).

> *Weighted additive decision strategy*: The first strategy in this category is called *weighted additive decision strategy*, or *WADD*. The idea here is to assign weights to each attribute, and using those weights to compute an overall score for each alternative. You select the one with the best score of the pair.
>
> For example, let us assume that you want to consider just two attributes: distance to the warehouse and the distance to the plant. You assign distance to the plant a weight of 70 per cent and distance to the warehouse a weight of 30 per cent. Your score for supplier #1 would be $0.70 \times 60 + 0.30 \times 100 = 42 + 30 = 72$. Your score for supplier #2 would be $0.70 \times 40 + 0.30 \times 130 = 28 + 39 = 67$. Supplier #2 would be better than supplier #1 because in this case the best score is the lowest score (the lesser the distance to the warehouse and the plant the better). Note that supplier #2 is futher away from the warehouse than supplier #1, but it is closer to the plant and this compensates

sufficiently. Had you selected different weights, for example, 30 per cent for the plant and 70 per cent for the warehouse, supplier #1 would have come on top.

You cannot apply the WADD strategy to interval, ordinal, or nominal scales. This is because you need to be able to add and multiply the attribute values and therefore these values need to be of ratio scale. To take attributes with other scales into account you would first need to map each of the attribute values to a utility using a utility function. After this you would be able to carry out the WADD strategy on the utilities. Information systems can be of great assistance here, and I shall be discussing the calculations of utilities at length a bit later on in this chapter, in Section 8.5.

Equal weights decision strategy or *EQW*: This is a simplified version of the WADD strategy in that each attribute is assumed to carry an equal weight. In this case, you would not need to assign weights for each attribute. For each alternative, you would sum up the utility of each value and the alternative with the best score wins.

Take, for example, distance to the plant and the warehouse again. Supplier #1 has a score of $60 + 100 = 160$ m. supplier #2 has a score of $40 + 130 = 170$ m. Thus, you would prefer supplier #1 in the EQW scenario. Note that you would have preferred supplier #2 in the WADD scenario!

Additive difference strategy: The third one is called *additive difference*, or ADIFF. The idea here is to add up differences and produce difference scores. For example, the difference in distance to the plant between supplier #1 and supplier #2 is -20 m. The difference in distance to warehouse between supplier #1 and supplier #2 is $+30$ m. The difference score is $0.70 \cdot -20 + 0.30 \cdot 30 = -14 + 9 = -5$ m. Or in other words, supplier #2 is -5 m better than supplier #1. It is a negative difference which is good in this case because the lesser the distance the better it is. Note that even though you compute the scores differently, it is very similar to WADD, and produces similar outcomes.

Majority of confirming dimensions: The fourth one, *majority of confirming dimensions*, or *MCD*, is a variant of the ADIFF strategy, simplified to make it applicable to ordinal and non-commensurable scales. Starting off with the first pairwise comparison, you would count the number of attributes that an alternative is better than the next one. You would also count the number of attributes that an alternative is worse than the next one. If the number of better alternatives is in the majority then you would proceed with the next one.

Satisficing: The fifth strategy is called the *satisficing decision strategy*, or *SAT*. The term satisficing was coined by Herbert Simon to describe the type of decisions in which we do not aim to select an alternative that is the 'best', but rather one that is 'good enough' (Simon 1955). When an alternative is 'good enough' for us, we tend to stop looking for better options. This strategy is called satisficing because it reflects exactly this. You would first define threshold levels (or cut-off levels) for each attribute.

Let us define, for example, cut-off levels for our supplier table. Let us assume any distance to plant or centre of 120 would be good enough, as would any price below 150. We would be satisfied with three-star material. The region would not matter. In that case the first supplier that meets all our threshold values in supplier #5.

Note that using a satisficing strategy, you run the risk of missing out on a better alternative. In the example above, supplier #6 also meets the threshold values, and it is arguable better than supplier #5. It is indeed unfortunate for supplier #6, because he or she was not first in the list of 'good enough' suppliers. You will note how important the order of the alternatives is if you adopt the satisficing approach.

You will also note that the SAT strategy is not based on pairwise comparisons, but rather on a comparison against a certain threshold or cut-off level. Another difference with the previous three strategies is that you do not need to evaluate all 12 alternatives before you make up your mind.

Frequency of good and bad features: The sixth strategy, *frequency of good and bad features* is an extension of the SAT decision strategy. Like this strategy, you would first define cut-off values for each attribute. But rather than deciding if attributes meet those values, you would count the number of positive attributes, and pass through each of the alternatives to see if that number increased.

Lexicographic: So far, all decision strategies were alternative-based. This means that you tend to look at each alternative, examine the attributes of interest and then decide on the value of the alternative. In terms of the decision matrix, you tend to have a 'row' view. The remaining two strategies are attribute-based. This means that you first examine the attributes, or, in other words, you tend to assume a 'column' view.

The first attribute-based strategy is called the *lexicographic* strategy, or *LEX*. This strategy follows the following procedure. First you decide on your most important attribute. You then select the top alternative on this attribute. If there are two or more competing alternatives, you proceed with the next most important attribute. From the subset of available 'top' attributes you would then select the top alternative on the next best attribute. And then so on until you have found your best alternative.

For example, suppose your top attribute would be quality. In that case you select all suppliers with the best quality, which are supplier #3, #6, and #8. You next select your second-most important attribute. This could be distance to the warehouse. This leaves you with supplier #8.

Elimination by aspect: The eighth and last decision strategy is called *elimination by aspect*, or *EBA*. The term 'aspect' is synonymous with attribute. This strategy, introduced by Tversky (1972), combines elements of the satisficing strategy and the lexicographic strategy. Like the lexicographic strategy, it looks at the attributes first and ranks these in order of importance. Like the satisficing strategy, it then eliminates alternatives using threshold values. With the EBA strategy, you would look at each attribute and eliminate all unattractive alternatives at once. With the satisficing strategy, you would look at each alternative one at a time and move on to the next if the alternative contained an unattractive attribute value.

In the supplier example, imagine that the most important attribute for you is price. You would then define your threshold level: this could be 60. This leaves you with supplier #7, #8, #9, and #12. You then select your next important attribute: this could be quality. You would want at least a three-star. This cut-off value is applied to the remaining two and you are left with supplier #8.

Table 8.2 Eight decision strategies (Payne et al. 1993)

	Decision strategy	Alternative or attribute based	Scales	Compensatory	Threshold
1	WADD	Alternative	Ratio	Yes	No
3	EQW	Alternative	Ratio	Yes	No
2	ADDIF	Alternative	Ratio	Yes	No
4	MCD	Alternative	Ordinal	Yes	No
6	SAT	Alternative	Ordinal	No	Yes
5	FRQ	Alternative	Ordinal	Yes	Yes
7	LEX	Attribute	Ordinal	No	No
8	EBA	Attribute	Ordinal	No	Yes

Table 8.2 presents an overview of the eight decision strategies.

As we have seen, some decision strategies do not take into account all attribute values of a single alternative. That is, the strategy never really considers any potential trade-offs, whether one value (quality) could compensate for another value (price). These strategies are called *non-compensatory*. EBA, LEX, and SAT are non-compensatory strategies.

You apply a *compensatory strategy* if you look at one attribute of an alternative under the assumption that it can offset another. In other words, if you look at two attributes of one alternative, an attractive value on one attribute can compensate for an unattractive value on another attribute. WADD, EQW, ADIFF, MCD, and FRQ are compensatory strategies.

When faced with large numbers of alternatives, people tend to start off with non-compensatory strategies. They do so to *simplify*, to bring the number of alternatives down to a manageable set. When the set of alternatives is sufficiently small, people begin to study that smaller set in more detail, and start to apply compensatory strategies. The name for this subset of alternatives is *consideration set* (Shocker et al. 1991).

The consideration set is not usually large, and is typically limited to five or six. Furthermore, it has been posited that the reason why people form consideration sets is that they are refusing to evaluate more alternatives than they can mentally cope with (Hauser and Wernerfelt 1990). This is reminiscent of the information overload discussion from Chapter 1.

The decision strategies that I have described can be decomposed into sequences of smaller steps: looking at an attribute value, comparing this value with another attribute value, storing the value, and so on. We can conceptualize these steps as building blocks, from which higher-level decision strategies can be constructed. Such building blocks are called *Elementary Information Processing* units, or *EIPs* (Newell and Simon 1972).

If you add up the number of EIPs for each decision strategy, you will see that some decision strategies require much less EIPs than others (Johnson and Payne 1985; Payne, Bettman, and Johnson 1988). The EBA strategy, for example, is able to discard an alternative by looking at one attribute only. The WADD strategy cannot do that: it needs to evaluate all the other attributes to see if any one of them might offset that value.

The number of EIPs are a measure of cognitive *effort* and therefore we can say that some decision strategies require less effort than others. As a general heuristic, we could say that the non-compensatory strategies require less effort than the compensatory strategies.

Decision strategies also vary in their level of *accuracy*. Accuracy is usually measured as the amount of information that is processed in a decision. For example, EBA is less accurate than WADD because, for each alternative, EBA only processes one attribute value whereas WADD processes all the attribute values. The SAT strategy, another non-compensatory strategy, is not the most accurate because it discards any alternative that can be better than the chosen one. As a general heuristic, we could say the compensatory strategies are more accurate than the non-compensatory strategies.

The implication is that strategies with the highest accuracy incur the most effort! Choosing a decision strategy is therefore the result of a trade-off: balancing accuracy with the effort required to achieve that accuracy. The choice of decision strategy is a function of the user's expectation of the effort spent as well as the user's expectation of the accuracy gained. Expected effort and accuracy are in turn determined by a number of other factors, which are discussed more fully by Payne (1982).

Please be aware that the format of the decision matrix is a key design problem for this type of decision. It is clear that the type of display can facilitate or complicate the application of certain decision strategies (Kleinmuntz and Schkade 1993). Tversky (1972) noted that attribute-based strategies can only be effective if the attributes are organized in columns for ease of comparison. The order of the attributes and the order of the alternatives can have a dramatic impact on the alternative that is eventually selected by the user, and this means that the design of the decision matrix requires your careful attention.

8.4. **Shortlisting**

A technique to support managers in this type of decisions is *shortlisting*. Systems that implement this technique will allow the user to create a short-list from the larger set of alternatives that are available. The system would allow the user to swap back and forth between the alternative set and the consideration set, and to add and subtract alternatives from the alternative set to the consideration set.

The shortlisting technique can be implemented in a variety of ways, the most obvious of which is to allow the user to maintain two different decision matrices: one with the alternative set and one with the consideration set. The well-known online bookstore Amazon, along with many other online retailers, implemented this through the introduction of the *wish list*.

Another way of implementing the shortlisting technique is to allow the user to flag an alternative for further consideration. In this case no separate list is maintained, but an alternative is clearly labelled as being part of a separate list. Isolation techniques can be used to make those alternatives stand out from the other ones: for example, shortlisted alternatives could have a different foreground or background colour, they could be blinking, and so on.

When alternatives are flagged for consideration it can be helpful to order the alternative set according to 'flagged status' so that the flagged alternatives come out on top. This would be helpful because alternatives need to be grouped together to facilitate the application of attribute-based decision strategies. Combining this technique with the manipulation technique would allow the user to order the flagged alternatives in the main decision matrix.

An information system that applied the shortlisting techniques would display the decision matrix to the user, offer an opportunity to rank the alternatives, and form a consideration set out of them. This assumes that the user is able and willing to look at each alternative individually. On many occasions this is not the case. Sometimes the user may not be willing to look at each alternative individually. This occurs, for example, when the user is under time pressure. Other times the alternative set may simply be too large to evaluate. There may not be 12 suppliers to choose from, but 12,000 if your search is not particularly restrictive.

Table 8.3 Examples of conditional selection

Attribute	Scale	Example
Region	Nominal	Select if region A
Quality	Ordinal	Select if 3 star or higher
Distance	Ratio	Select if less than 40m from plant or city
Price	Ratio	Select if less than 200 euros

To help create an automatic shortlist, *conditional selection* can be used. The idea is to offer the user a number of cut-off levels to eliminate a number of alternatives from the decision matrix. The information system cuts out alternatives that the user thinks are below or above certain thresholds. In spreadsheet software this function is available under the name *filter* or *autofilter*.

Take for example Table 8.1. Rather than presenting the matrix directly, an information system could ask the user to select an alternative by region, by quality rating, or by distance to plant and warehouse. Table 8.3 provides examples of such conditional selection.

Table 8.3 illustrates how conditional selection is different for nominal, ordinal, interval, and ratio-scales. If you have a nominal scale, the user would have to mention one or more nominal values to ascertain which alternative is going to be selected or not. For ordinal scales and above, you can specify cut-off levels (at least three star for example).

It is often useful to depict the number of alternatives for each available shortlist in brackets. For example, 'Select at least three-star suppliers (6)' would indicate that if the user selects this option, he or she would be left with six suppliers. The option 'Select at least four-star alternatives (3)' would indicate that the user would be left with three suppliers. Providing the number of alternatives remaining after the conditional select will allow the user to help him or her to narrow down the matrix to a comfortable consideration set of alternatives.

Note how the conditional select is particularly useful in supporting elimination strategies. It supports the SAT and EBA strategies because it looks at the user thresholds and reduces the matrix to only those alternatives that satisfy the cut-off values. Elsewhere this technique has also been called conditional elimination, or conditional drop (Todd and Benbasat 1992), to illustrate how effective it is in supporting elimination strategies.

Conditional selection works on the assumption that the user will be able to specify cut-off values: thresholds that define whether an alternative is ready for shortlisting. In a similar vein, the information system itself may notify the user which alternative may be worth considering. I call this feature *cueing*, because the system is aiming to give the user a cue as to which alternative they might like.

An example of cueing could be cueing by 'dominance'. An alternative *dominates* another alternative if it performs equally well or better on all attributes that are at least ordinal scaled. For example, in Table 8.1 supplier #9 'dominates' supplier #12. The system could provide a cue that would point out if an alternative was dominant or not. Or it could point out for certain alternatives another dominant alternative is available.

8.5. **Utility mapping**

Apart from shortlisting there is second technique that can help managers in selecting alternatives. This technique is called *utility mapping* (Keeney and Raiffa 1976). The idea here is to create a new list of alternatives, in order of user preference. You derive this ordered list by modelling the preferences of the user, matching those preferences with the attribute values of the alternative, and calculating an overall *utility*. This is a score that indicates to the user the extent to which the alternative would be interesting. A system can use the overall utility to rank order the alternatives.

Note how very close this technique is to the WADD strategy. Essentially, the system attempts to carry out the WADD strategy on behalf of the user. Note also that utility mapping is a bit like cueing, in that it also recommends alternatives to the user. The difference is that the cue is nominal and the utility is ratio. The cue tells the user that the alternative is either interesting or uninteresting, to be included in the shortlist or not. With utility mapping, the system can tell the user the *extent* to which the alternative might be interesting.

The creation of the overall utility is not a trivial process, and I will now discuss its derivation in more detail. The process involves two steps. First, you need to define utility functions for each of the attributes, mapping each value to a utility. Note how you need to perform this step because

Table 8.4 Utility mappings

#	Attribute	Utility function U
1	Region	$U1 = 0$ if region A $U1 = 100$ if region B
2	Quality	$U2 = 0$ if 2 star $U2 = 50$ if 3 star $U3 = 100$ if 4 star
3	Distance	$U3, U4 = $ (highest distance − distance) / highest distance × 100
4	Price	$U5 = $ (highest price − price) / price × 100

the attributes are not directly comparable to each other. The second step is to add a weight to each of the attributes. You can then create a weighted average score that takes into account all the attributes.

Let us put this to the test with an example, and let us again take the supplier list from Table 8.1. First, I am going to define a utility function for each attribute. I will then examine the preferences for each of the attributes. Table 8.4 displays a set of utility functions.

Let us have a look at each of the utility functions. Notice first how each function maps the attribute values to a utility between 0 and 100. This lower bound of 0 and upper bound of 100 is completely arbitrary, and I might have picked any other set of numbers, −3 to +3 for example. But if you have decided on the upper and lower bound of these utilities, you need to stick to them throughout your attribute mapping. Do not be tempted to prevent an attribute to score the full 100 points. If you do so, you are not giving that attribute a fair chance in the second step, where the weighting takes place. If you want to discount that attribute, you can do so when you consider the weighting in the second step.

Notice also the different types of each of the functions. To map the nominal values to utilities, you would use what is known in mathematics as a step function, that is, one value for each step (attribute value). To map the ordinal values, you could either use a step function, with each value a higher utility, or use a discrete function, one that takes the rank number as the independent value. Finally, metric values can take step, discrete, and continuous functions. Note also how I have turned the utility mapping around for distance and price: the lower the distance and the lower the price, the higher the utility.

Table 8.5 Calculating the utility (*U*)

#	Region	Rating	Distance to plant	Distance to warehouse	Price	*U*
1	0	0	85	33	40	29.8
2	100	50	90	13	50	60.5
3	100	100	75	0	0	51.3
4	0	0	0	27	65	23.5
5	0	50	88	33	25	35.6
6	100	100	88	7	50	69.1
7	100	0	50	67	80	61.5
8	0	100	75	27	80	59.3
9	0	0	25	33	85	34.3
10	100	50	0	27	65	53.5
11	0	0	50	50	60	33.0
12	0	0	25	27	75	30.3

Now for the second step. Suppose that distance and price are the most important criteria for the user, and the other criteria are somewhat less important. This would be reflected by a weighting of 20 per cent for interior, 20 per cent for quality, 15 per cent for plant and city distance each, and 30 per cent of the price. Thus the score for each alternative is going to be

$$U = 0.20 \times U1 + 0.20 \times U2 + 0.15 \times U3 + 0.15 \times U4 + 0.30 \times U5$$

The result would be a scoring table as in Table 8.5.

And using the total utility, the system can produce an ordered list of the suppliers as in Table 8.6. I have here used a display where I have ordered the alternatives such that the number one came first, followed by the second one, and so on. The disadvantage of this is that the distances between the alternatives are lost. Fortunately, there are other ways of displaying the data.

In terms of display, I could also leave the list unordered, and single out shortlisted alternatives in other ways. Examples include a shaded background, for example, a green background if the alternative was interesting, and a red one if it was not. For ordinal scales, I could introduce colour shades. If the scale was metric (ordinal or ratio), I could use the data in the index to match the colour shade. Finally, I have also seen displays where the alternatives are displayed in a 'cloud', and the size of the font in which the supplier was displayed would correspond with the score that it was associated with.

Table 8.6 Suppliers ranked by utility

#	Region	Rating	Distance to plant	Distance to warehouse	Price
6	Region B	4 star	50	140	100
7	Region B	2 star	200	50	40
2	Region A	3 star	40	130	100
8	Region A	4 star	100	110	40
10	Region B	3 star	400	110	70
3	Region B	4 star	100	150	200
5	Region A	3 star	50	100	150
9	Region A	2 star	300	100	30
11	Region A	2 star	200	75	80
12	Region A	2 star	300	110	50
1	Region A	2 star	60	100	120
4	Region A	2 star	400	110	70

Shortlisting and utility mapping can of course be combined. In that case, the system could create a consideration set for the user by setting a threshold utility (e.g. 75) and putting all the alternatives which exceed this threshold in the consideration set. Häubl and Trifts (2000) report a study where they implemented such a decision aid. They found that users that had access to this tool had obtained lower search effort and better decision accuracy than those that did not have access.

☐ FURTHER READING

This chapter has focused on the design of information systems for a specific decision: to select an alternative out of a set of available candidates. We have seen how a number of decision strategies are available. Eight strategies were discussed, compensatory and non-compensatory. The strategies differ in the amount of effort lost and the amount of decision accuracy gained, and choosing a strategy is a function of the anticipated effort and accuracy. People tend to form a consideration set midway during the decision process, with non-compensatory strategies leading up to set formation, and compensatory strategies used to make the final decision.

Researchers have been studying different information displays, and the effects that these different displays have on the nature of decision-making. Payne (1982) cites a number of such studies. Studies by Todd and Benbasat (1991, 1992, 1999) provide further insight in the role that information systems play in improving management decision-making. I have also published some research in this area myself (van der Heijden 2006).

A final word of caution: when you design an information system to help you select an alternative, you must be acutely aware of a concept called *decisional guidance*. If the system preselects the information based on certain conditions, or if it ranks the alternatives based on a utility function that may not accurately reflect your own, the system will guide you towards certain alternatives even though there may have been other ones in the alternative set that you would find superior. For a thorough discussion on this, see Silver (1991).

9 Epilogue

In this book, I have set out to address key managerial skills that are needed to design management information systems. We have looked at the structuring of data first, followed by the querying of data, and finally data aggregation and visualization. We then discussed two types of management decisions, and I demonstrated how the design skills could be put to use in order to support those decisions.

Having read this book, you may find it a useful exercise to re-read the book 'in reverse'. That would imply starting with the management decisions, and then moving backwards to see how the management information that is needed to support those decisions is actually shaped. For a manager, this will often be the way to approach the design of the management information system, that is, starting at the tail end of the process with a sketch of the management report. For a management information system designer, the approach will more likely be from the other direction, for example, starting with a sketch of the data model. In any case, managers and designers alike are advised to study both directions, as they will have to find ways to 'meet in the middle.'

In writing this book, I realize that I have only touched the surface of the vast material that is available on MIS design. There is a great deal more to read and study about the structuring of data, the querying of data, the aggregation of data, and the visualization of data. Similarly, there is more to say about the two management decisions that I have covered at the end of the book, monitoring key performance indicators and selecting alternatives. I have aimed to provide an overview of the design of management information systems, with references to more detailed literature should you want to study aspects of it in more depth.

In this epilogue, I should like to touch on three aspects of designing management information systems that I have not discussed so far. These aspects are important enough to be mentioned here, even though the book itself did not cover them in great detail.

Data quality: A recurring issue in the extraction of data from source systems is *data quality*. You will appreciate that the quality of data from the management information system is entirely dependent on the quality of data from the source systems. If that data is inaccurate, not sufficiently precise, incomplete, or outdated, so will be the data from the management information systems. This is encapsulated in the well-known mantra *Garbage In, Garbage Out*. If managers do not trust the data put in front of them, the system that provides the data will effectively be useless, no matter how long it took to develop and no matter how expensive it was. Data quality is the Achilles heel of any management information system, and the preservation of data quality from the source systems should be an elementary designer's concern.

Management consensus: I have more or less assumed in the writing of this book that designing a management information system is an individual exercise. Many information systems, however, are designed by teams, and often large teams at that. In addition, the systems are used by more than one manager, and not every manager has the same requirements for specific management information. This means that often we cannot ignore the teamwork aspects of designing information systems, and that consensus building (and indeed negotiating) is often part of the design process. Designing in teams is often rewarding and exciting, with many stakeholders bringing their specific interests to the table. I should note that it can occasionally be challenging as well, as stakeholder interests cannot always be completely reconciled.

Politics: Finally, I have excluded at least one dimension in the course of this book: the political. I mention it here because it would be naive to assume that designing management information systems can somehow be disconnected from politics. Most managers will quickly concede that politics play an important part in their organizations, and that management information is often used as part of the political game—to be emphasized when favourable, to be glossed over when unfavourable. Management information systems often monitor human behaviour, with employees capturing transactions that reveal their performance at least to some extent. Disclosing behaviour to others is traditionally sensitive and provides many fruitful avenues for political manoeuvering.

It is important to recognize that all three aspects are of vital importance for the successful completion of a management information system. No system can be useful without it addressing the issues of data quality, management consensus, and politics. Covering these topics in this book, however, would not have done them justice. They require a great deal more coverage than this book would have been able to provide. Indeed, one could say there is a separate book to be written on all three topics.

Many academic scholars in management information systems are concerned precisely with these matters, as they so often provide stumbling blocks for successful management information systems to materialize. For the latest research on these and other topics in management information systems, it is worthwhile to read academic journals in this area. The following three are well known: MIS Quarterly, Information Systems Research, and the European Journal of Information Systems. The articles in these journals are not always squarely targeted at the average manager (they usually have an academic audience in mind), but studying them can nonetheless be a rewarding and intellectually stimulating exercise. I would encourage you to take a look at these journals for more in-depth study.

Regardless of whether you want to delve into MIS areas in more depth, if you have studied this book to the end, I am confident that you will have become a better MIS designer. If you then proceed by using your own management information systems, it is my modest hope that you will also be a better manager.

☐ APPENDIX 1 TRANSACTION DATA FOR SALES DEPARTMENT CASE

The following R-tables represent fictional data for the sales department case. They form the basis for the de-normalized data set that was created in Chapter 4 (Table 4.1 on page 61).

Product Category

```
category_id name
=========== ========
1           Food
2           Non-Food
```

Product

```
product_id name    price category_id
=========== ====== ===== ============
1           Orange  1    1
2           Soap    5    2
3           Wine    10   1
4           Apple   1    1
5           Candle  7    2
```

Customer Status

```
status_id name             rank
========= =============== ====
1         Contact          1
2         Lead             2
3         Promising Lead   3
4         Prospect         4
5         Customer         5
```

Customer

```
customer_id name    status_id
=========== ======= =========
1           Cyndi   5
2           Kasey   5
3           Evelyne 5
4           Ocean   5
5           Joan    5
6           Myra    5
7           Godfrey 5
8           Celeste 5
9           Lennard 5
10          Justin  5
```

Sales Team

```
team_id name
======= =====
1       Alpha
2       Beta
3       Gamma
```

Sales Agent

```
agent_id name on_probation team_id
======== ==== ============ =======
1        Jim  true         1
2        Tom  true         2
3        Mary false        1
4        Jim  false        2
5        Jack false        NULL
```

Order

order_id	customer_id	agent_id	date
1	1	1	3 Jan
2	2	3	7 Jan
3	3	2	8 Jan
4	4	1	9 Jan
5	5	4	11 Jan
6	6	3	15 Jan
7	7	2	17 Jan
8	8	3	21 Jan
9	9	4	29 Jan
10	10	2	30 Jan

Line Item

item_id	order_id	product_id	quantity
1	1	1	6
2	1	5	34
3	2	3	24
4	2	1	4
5	2	4	35
6	3	1	13
7	3	2	19
8	4	4	30
9	4	2	9
10	5	2	14
11	5	3	16
12	6	4	21
13	6	1	8
14	7	5	33
15	8	3	20
16	8	5	32
17	9	4	26
18	10	2	15
19	10	3	17
20	10	5	7

☐ REFERENCES

Ackoff, R. L. (1967). Management misinformation systems. *Management Science, 14*(4), 147–56.

Albers, J. (2006). *Interaction of Color* (Rev Exp edn.). New Haven, CT: Yale University Press.

Allport, D. A. (1980). Attention and performance. In G. Claxton (ed.), *Cognitive Psychology.* London: Routledge and Kegan Paul.

Barker, R. (1989). *Case*Method—Entity Relationship Modelling.* Wokingham, England: Addison-Wesley.

Becker, Richard A. and Cleveland, William S. (1987, May). Brushing scatterplots. *Technometrics, 29*(2), 127–42.

Benbasat, I. and Dexter, A. S. (1986). An investigation of the effectiveness of colour and graphical information presentation under varying time constraints. *MIS Quarterly*(March), 59–83.

Benbasat, I. and Schroeder, R. G. (1977). An experimental investigation of some MIS design variables. *MIS Quarterly*(March), 37–49.

Berenson, M. L., Levine, D., and Krehbiel, T. C. (2005). *Basic Business Statistics: Concepts and Applications* (10th edn.). Upper Saddle River, NJ: Prentice-Hall.

Booch, G. (1993). *Obect-Oriented Analysis and Design with Applications.* Redwood City: Benjamin-Cunnings.

——— Rumbaugh, J., and Jacobsen, I. (1999). *The Unified Modeling Language User Guide.* Upper Saddle River, NJ: Addison-Wesley.

Chen, P. P.*-S. (1976). The entity-relationship model—toward a unified view of data. *ACM Transactions on Database Systems, 1*(1), 9–36.

Chernoff, H. (1973). The use of faces to represent points in k-dimensional space graphically. *Journal of the American Statistical Association, 68*(342), 361–8.

Chervany, N. and Dickson, G. (1974). An experimental evaluation of information overload in a production environment. *Management Science* (10), 1335–44.

Cleveland, W. S. (1985). *The Elements of Graphic Data.* Murray Hill, NJ: Bell Telephone Laboratories.

——— (1993). *Visualizing Data.* Murray Hill, NJ: AT&T Bell Laboratories.

Codd, E. F. (1970). A relational model of data for large shared data banks. *Communications of the ACM, 13*(6), 377–87.

Date, C. (2000). *An Introduction to Database Systems* (7th edn.). Reading, MA: Addison-Wesley.

Dickson, G. W., Senn, J. A., and Chervany, N. L. (1977). Research in management information systems: the Minnesota experiments. *Management Science, 23*(9), 913–23.

Drucker, P. (1995). The information executives truly need. *Harvard Business Review* (January–February), 55–62.

Few, S. (2006). *Information Dashboard Design: The Effective Visual Communication of Data.* Sebastopol, CA: O'Reilly.

Fowler, M. (2004). *UML Distilled: A Brief Guide to the Standard Object Modeling Language* (3rd edn.). Boston, MA: Addison-Wesley.

Haag, S., Cummings, M., and Phillips, A. (2007). *Management Information Systems for the Information Age* (6th edn.). New York: McGraw-Hill/Irwin.

Harris, R. L. (1999). *Information Graphics: A Comprehensive Illustrated Reference.* Oxford: Oxford University Press.

Häubl, G. and Trifts, V. (2000). Consumer decision making in online shopping environments: the effects of interactive decision aids. *Marketing Science, 19*(1), 4–21.

Hauser, J. R. and Wernerfelt, B. (1990). An evaluation cost model of consideration sets. *Journal of Consumer Research, 16*(March), 393–408.

Huff, D. (1991). *How to Lie with Statistics* (New edn.). London: Penguin Books.

Jacobson, I. (1992). *Object-Oriented Software Engineering: A Use Case Driven Approach.* Upper Saddle River, NJ: Addison-Wesley.

Johnson, E. J. and Payne, J. W. (1985). Effort and accuracy in choice. *Management Science, 31*(4), 395–414.

Kahneman, D. (1973). *Attention and Effort.* Englewood Cliffs, NJ: Prentice Hall.

Kaplan, R. S. and Norton, D. P. (1996). *The Balanced Scorecard: Translating Strategy into Action.* Boston, MA: Harvard Business School Press.

Keeney, R. L. and Raiffa, H. (1976). *Decisions with Multiple Objectives: Preferences and Value Tradeoffs.* New York: John Wiley and Sons.

Kendall, K. E. and Kendall, J. E. (1999). *Systems Analysis and Design* (4th edn.). Upper Saddle River, NJ: Prentice Hall.

Kleinmuntz, D. N. and Schkade, D. A. (1993). Information displays and decision processes. *Psychological Science, 4*(4), 221–7.

Laudon, K. C. and Laudon, J. P. (2004). *Management Information Systems: Managing the Digital Firm* (8th edn.). Upper Saddle River, NJ: Prentice Hall.

Miller, G. A. (1956). The magical number seven, plus or minus two: some limits on our capacity for processing information. *Psychological Review, 63*, 81–97.

Newell, A. and Simon, H. A. (1972). *Human Problem Solving.* Englewood Cliffs, NJ: Prentice-Hall.

Norman, D. A. and Bobrow, D. G. (1975). On data-limited and resource-limited processes. *Cognitive Psychology, 7*, 44–64.

O'Brien, J. A. and Marakas, G. M. (2006). *Management Information Systems* (7th edn.). New York: McGraw-Hill/Irwin.

Payne, J., Bettman, J., and Johnson, E. (1993). *The Adaptive Decision Maker*. New York: Cambridge University Press.

Payne, J. W. (1982). Contingent decision behavior. *Psychological Bulletin, 92*(2), 382–402.

——Bettman, J. R., and Johnson, E. J. (1988). Adaptive strategy selection in decision making. *Journal of Experimental Psychology: Learning, Memory, and Cognition, 14*(3), 534–52.

Pollack, I. (1952). The information of elementary auditory displays. *Journal of the Acoustical Society of America, 24*(6), 745–9.

Powsner, S. M. and Tufte, E. R. (1994, August). Graphical summary of patient status. *The Lancet, 344*, 386–9.

Rumbaugh, J., Blaha, M., Premerlani, W., Eddy, F., and Lorensen, W. (1991). *Object-Oriented Modeling and Design*. Upper Saddle River, NJ, USA: Prentice-Hall.

——Booch, G., and Jacobson, I. (1999). *The Unified Modeling Language Reference Manual*. Upper Saddle River, NJ: Addison-Wesley.

Saunders, M., Lewis, P., and Thornhill, A. (2006). *Research Methods for Business Students* (4th edn.). Harlow: Prentice Hall, Financial Times.

Shiffrin, R. M. and Nosofsky, R. M. (1994). Seven plus or minus two: a commentary on capacity limitations. *Psychological Review, 101*(2), 357–61.

Shocker, A. D., Ben-Akiva, M., Boccara, B., and Nedungadi, P. (1991). Consideration set influences on consumer decision making and choice: issues, models, and suggestions. *Marketing Letters, 2*(3), 181–97.

Silver, M. S. (1991). Decisional guidance for computer-based decision support. *MIS Quarterly* (March), 105–22.

Simon, H. A. (1955). A behavioral model of rational choice. *Quarterly Journal of Economics, 69*, 99–118.

——(1971). Designing organizations for an information-rich world. In M. Greenberger (ed.), *Computers, Communications and the Public Interest*. Baltimore, MD: John Hopkins Press.

——(1974). How big is a chunk? *Science, 183*(4124), 482–8.

Spence, R. (2007). *Information Visualization: Design for Interaction* (2nd edn.). Essex: Pearson Education.

Stevens, S. (1946). On the theory of scales of measurement. *Science, 103*, 677–80.

Styles, E. A. (2006). *The Psychology of Attention* (2nd edn.). Hove: Psychology Press.

Svenson, O. (1979). Process descriptions of decision making. *Organizational Behavior and Human Performance, 23*, 86–112.

Todd, P. and Benbasat, I. (1991). An experimental investigation of the impact of computer based decision aids on decision making strategies. *Information Systems Research*, 2(2), 87–115.

—— —— (1992). The use of information in decison making: an experimental investigation of the impact of computer-based decision aids. *MIS Quarterly* (September), 373–93.

—— —— (1999). Evaluating the impact of DSS, cognitive effort, and incentives on strategy selection. *Information Systems Research*, 10(4), 356–74.

Tufte, E. R. (1983). *The Visual Display of Quantitative Information*. Cheshire: Graphics Press.

Tukey, J. W. (1977). *Exploratory Data Analysis*. Reading, MA: Addison-Wesley.

Tversky, A. (1972). Elimination by aspects: a theory of choice. *Psychological Review*, 79(4), 281–99.

van der Heijden, H. (2006). Mobile decision support for in-store purchase decisions. *Decision Support Systems*, 42(2), 656–63.

van der Lans, R. F. (1989). *The SQL Standard: A Complete Reference*. Hemel Hempstead: Prentice Hall International.

Ware, C. (2004). *Information Visualization: Perception for Design*. San Francisco: Morgan Kaufmann, Elsevier.

Wildbur, P. and Burke, M. (1998). *Information Graphics*. London: Thames and Hudson.

☐ INDEX